Rethinking Morphology

Rethinking Morphology

Laurie Bauer

EDINBURGH
University Press

Edinburgh University Press is one of the leading university presses in the UK. We publish academic books and journals in our selected subject areas across the humanities and social sciences, combining cutting-edge scholarship with high editorial and production values to produce academic works of lasting importance. For more information visit our website: edinburghuniversitypress.com

Edinburgh University Press Ltd
The Tun – Holyrood Road, 12(2f) Jackson's Entry, Edinburgh
EH8 8PJ

Typeset in 10.5/12pt Janson MT by
Servis Filmsetting Ltd, Stockport, Cheshire
and printed and bound in Great Britain.

A CIP record for this book is available from the British Library

ISBN 978 1 4744 3615 1 (hardback)
ISBN 978 1 4744 3616 8 (paperback)
ISBN 978 1 4744 3617 5 (webready PDF)
ISBN 978 1 4744 3618 2 (epub)

Contents

Acknowledgements

In 1991, I was asked to write a review of Becker (1990), a review which appeared as Bauer (1993). In Becker's book, he advocates an approach to word-formation based on analogy rather than on rules. At the time, I genuinely could not see how his proposals provided an improvement over the rule-based systems that were the norm at the time, or what his analogies were. The review I wrote was correspondingly critical. However, over the following years, my students were very enthusiastic about Becker's approach, and I found myself unable to convince them that there was any downside to what he was doing. It has taken me over twenty years to come round to something that is more like Becker's approach and less like the one with which I was operating in the early 1990s. In this, I probably show myself to be akin to those recording labels that turned down the Beatles and the publishers who refused to publish the works of J. K. Rowling. I was certainly slow on the uptake, and I feel I owe a belated apology to Becker who was, in 1990, a prophet crying in the wilderness. I do not believe that I am the only one who has rethought their approach to morphology over the period since Becker's book was published. Cognitive approaches to linguistics have become far more widely promulgated and accepted in the community as a whole over that time. While I don't particularly think of myself as a cognitive linguist (and I feel fairly sure that real cognitive linguists would not see me as being one of their number), I have been affected by the cognitive strains in linguistics that have suffused the literature, and influenced not only me but also the students I have taught and authors of articles I have read. Having said that, this book is not Becker's book brought up to date, and is still based on ideas controversial enough to make it unlikely that everything proposed here will be welcomed in the morphological community. So be it. That is why the word *rethinking* in the title is appropriate.

I should like to thank all of those who have supported me in various ways during the gestation of this book, introducing me to ideas that were revolutionary to me, and encouraging my work in other fora, which have helped the rethinking process. In particular, I should like to thank Natalia Beliaeva and Liza Tarasova who not only forced me to think of cognitive linguistics seriously, but also read an earlier draft of this book and commented helpfully on it. I should also like to thank the team at Edinburgh University Press, who welcomed me back into the fold, and encouraged improvements in the exposition, and my wife Winifred for showing me how to say what I meant to say. And this book would not be what it is without support from colleagues and friends at Victoria University, who answer innumerable stupid questions and keep me sane with entertaining conversation. The first draft of this book was written just after I retired after nearly forty years at Victoria, when I was enjoying the novelty of being an Emeritus Professor and having time free from administrative duties.

Abbreviations and notational conventions

1, 2, 3	first, second, third person
PL	plural
SG	singular
<. . .>	enclose spellings, or orthographic representations
/. . ./	enclose phonemes
[. . .]	enclose speech sounds; show features; mark morphological or syntactic constituents (bracketings)
italics	represent word-forms, morphs or words; mark mentioned words or expressions
SMALL CAPITALS	represent lexemes; represent morphological properties in glosses
'. . .'	enclose glosses; enclose technical terms when first introduced; mark quotations
{. . .}	enclose morphemes
°	indicates that the preceding word is in the glossary

1 Introduction

1.1 Morphology and the word

Morphology is the study of the meaningful structure of words. The word *cats* means what it means because it contains structural elements which, in construction° with each other, mean 'more than one cat'. On the other hand, there is nothing internal in *dog* which tells you what *dog* means. Even if we know that there is a contrasting word *hog*, the initial /d/ of *dog* does not provide the meaning 'canine'. Rather /d/ has no meaning by itself, but merely the ability to construct meanings when put together with other sounds. To put that another way, *dog* has phonological (and also orthographic°) structure, but no internal structure which is meaningful. It is analysable° from a phonological point of view, but not from a morphological point of view. An element like *dog* can be one of the building blocks of morphological analysis of a word like *doggy*, which is morphologically analysable°, but is itself not susceptible to morphological analysis.

There is a fundamental presupposition in the definition that has just been given, and that is that we can recognise (and preferably define) a 'word'. This is so far from being the truth that it is, in principle, a genuine problem for morphological study. For speakers of a language like English, with a long tradition of literacy, this may seem odd, because we are used to seeing words laid out on the page of print. But such a layout is purely convention: English as a language would not be fundamentally different ifwewroteitinthiskindofway. There are languages which are, or have been, written like that, from Ancient Greek to modern Thai. We would presumably not want to say that such languages do not have words. The implication is that the words we see on the page, the orthographic words°, are words by some kind of convention. Even in English, there are things which we do not know how to write in words. Is it *alright* or *all right*? Is it *in so far as* or *insofar as*? Is it *coffee pot* or *coffeepot*? There is variation in the way these are written in English, which is equivalent to saying that the conventions about words in English have fuzzy edges. These few examples are enough to show that any hard-and-fast definition of 'word', even in English, is likely to be problematic.

Like most books on morphology, this book will ignore the problem. It will be assumed that orthographic words represent 'words' in the more general sense, and the fuzzy-edge problems will be put to one side. This is far from ideal, but the only way of making any progress.

Having said that, there are several different kinds of words, and these are routinely distinguished by a standard terminology. Consider, first, the sentence in (1), attributed to Bernard Baruch:

(1) To me old age is always fifteen years older than I am.

In this sentence, is *old* the same word as *older* or are they different words? If you looked them up in a dictionary, they would both be given as part of the same entry, and in this sense they are the same word. Because this is to do with the dictionary (or lexical°) sense of 'word', we can call this idea of the word the 'lexeme°'. On the other hand, *older* has a different form from *old*; it has more letters (or phonemes°) in it. In that sense they are different words, and because this kind of word has to do with the shape, we will say they are different 'word-forms°'. If you were asked how many words of English you know, you would probably count *old* and *older* as the same word, and thus expect a count in terms of lexemes; if you were asked how long your essay was, you would count *old* and *older* in (1) as different words, and give a count of word-forms. We will need to return to this distinction in Chapter 3. It is usual to distinguish lexemes from word-forms in writing by using small capitals for lexemes and italics for word-forms, so that we can write: the lexeme OLD can be represented by the word-forms *old*, *older* and *oldest* (or, equivalently, but more economically, OLD can be represented by *old*, *older* and *oldest*). Where the distinction between lexeme and word-form is not critical, the term 'word°' will be used as a superordinate° term, and words, in this sense, will be italicised.

We will also need to make reference to the morphosyntactic word. The morphosyntactic word° is the word defined by its place in the grammatical system. The sentence in (2) is attributed to Mark Twain:

(2) Golf is a good walk spoiled.

Had Twain been English rather than American, he would probably have said *spoilt*. So there are two different word-forms which can have as their function 'the past participle of the verb SPOIL'. That is, a single morphosyntactic word can have two different word-forms to represent it. Also, a word-form like *spoiled* can either be the past tense of the verb

SPOIL or the past participle of the verb SPOIL, so that the same word-form can represent two different morphosyntactic words. In other words, even though a word-form like *cats* unambiguously represents the morphosyntactic word which we can gloss as 'the plural of CAT', there are enough cases where word-forms and morphosyntactic words do not align for the distinction to be crucial.

1.2 Theory and description

Every day, the sun rises in the east and sets in the west (with some variation depending upon latitude and time of year). That is a simple description of the facts, and is relatively straightforward. But if we want to know why that happens, we have to devise a theory of what is going on. We might have a theory that there is a huge supply of suns in the east, and every day one is fired across the sky and falls down in the west. If that were the case, we would expect to find a huge pile of used suns in the west, and we might go looking for that pile of suns to prove that our theory is right. Alternatively, we might look in the east for a pile of potential suns and some mechanism for firing them. An alternative theory might be that a god pulls the sun across the sky on a chariot every day. This would mean that there is only one sun, and so we would not expect to find piles of potential or discarded suns, but we would expect to find a way in which the sun could be returned to the east without shining on us. Or we might think that the sun revolves round the earth. Again, we have only one sun, but now we have to explain why the angle of the sun is different at different times of year according to a regular pattern. Or we might suggest that the earth revolves round the sun, not in a circle but in an ellipse, which has the added benefit of explaining the seasons (which adds external support to this theory). As we change our theoretical approach to the sun, we change the questions it is relevant to ask about the sun; we change the nature of the evidence which will support the theoretical stance we have taken; and in some sense we change what we see: a multitude of orbs being fired across the sky or the same orb returning; the movement of the sun or the movement of the earth. What we don't change is the observation that the sun rises in the east and sets in the west.

What is true of theories about the sun is true of other theories as well. Different theoretical views of what is going on in morphology will lead us to ask different questions and look for different kinds of evidence to support the theoretical views we support. But the fundamental observation is that a word like *dog* has only one chunk of meaning attached to it (however we wish to represent that meaning), while *cats* has two chunks of meaning associated with it, the meaning 'plural' or 'more than one' as well as the meaning 'cat'.

We are not concerned with questions of how to represent the meaning 'cat' in any greater detail here – that is a question for semanticists. It may be that the meaning 'cat' can be broken down into a number of semantic features° such as [animal] and [feline], or it may not. All that is crucial for morphologists is that the meaning 'cat' can be seen as a unitary element in the complexity of *cats*. If, in our study of morphology, we need more meaning than is available in the gloss 'cat', we can turn to standard dictionaries as a substitute for a semantic theory about how *cat* means 'cat', or what 'cat' involves.

What we are concerned with in this book is alternative theories about how the complexities of form and meaning in analysable° words like *cats* should be dealt with. Unfortunately, we are not in the position that astronomers find themselves in, in relation to their theory. After many centuries of evaluating theories about the sun, astronomers are now reasonably certain about the mechanisms involved in its apparent movement in relation to us. We are not in that position; in fact, we do not know at all how far we are from having any certainty about a theory of word-construction. At present, not only do we have multiple theories, it is also the case that we are uncertain about appropriate criteria for evaluating those theories. The result is that we may have to make assumptions about what makes one theory better than another. For instance, is a theory better the more closely it reflects the way native speakers deal with the structure in their heads? Alternatively, is a theory better if it is more economical, even if native speakers' heads have little use for economy? Different theories may make different assumptions about such matters, with the result that different theoretical structures will be proposed. In the final analysis, we do not know what 'the answer' is, or even if there is one. We hope to find that our theories will garner independent support along the way (like the explanation of the seasons, in the theories about the sun), which will provide encouragement that we may be on the right track. But if different theories appear to have different pieces of independent support, we will still have to evaluate our theories and decide which we prefer. Thus, even though linguists pride themselves on their adherence to scientific methodologies and the analysis of real data, there is also a metaphysics of linguistics, where we are looking for the most persuasive argument. In the end, you should have an idea about what might make a coherent story about morphological analysis; it is unlikely that we will hit upon the 'truth'.

1.3 About this book

This book is about the way we build theories about the structure of words. The observation is that some words appear to contain bits of form° which are related to predictable meaning. The theory is concerned with the system we see lying behind such relationships, the nature of the entities involved, and the arguments that might lead us to prefer one way of viewing the data over another. To do this, we need to go back to the very basics of morphology, so that some of what is said here might seem familiar or overly simple. Despite this return to the fundamentals, this is not primarily intended as a first book in linguistics. Some prior knowledge of linguistics and linguistic terminology is expected; this includes some familiarity with word-classes° (noun, verb, adjective, etc.) and some familiarity with phonetic transcription. This book is aimed at people who have had a brief introduction to morphology and want to know more, whether they need the information to do more linguistics, or to apply that knowledge to other fields of endeavour such as psychology, education or artificial intelligence; it is also intended to propose a new way of looking at morphological structure. All of this is implicit in the title, *Rethinking Morphology*. Because some readers may have less background than others, there is a glossary of linguistic terms (not just morphological terms). The definitions in the glossary are not meant to provide a full discussion of the terms involved, but simply to provide enough information for a reader who is insecure about the meaning or use of some term to continue to make progress. Terms that are listed in the glossary are followed by the symbol '°'. If there are readers who intend to use this book as a first introduction to linguistic morphology, they will need to make good use of the glossary, and will benefit from the support of a teacher or mentor. That is partly because, unlike truly introductory works, this book does not provide a single answer, but a series of arguments about what an answer might look like. The discussion topics are included to help people using this as a class text or for personal study come to grips with some of the issues involved, and the notion of discussion is important in this: different points of view may illuminate the issues. At the end of each chapter, there is also a section which draws attention to further sources, for people who want to extend their understanding of the material in the chapter. There is also a section of notes and comments on anything else that arises in the chapter but is not directly relevant to the argument presented in the chapter: alternative theoretical positions, questions left open in the chapter, wider implications, and the like.

Notes and comments

The view of words presented here is the distillation of a view which can be traced at least from Lyons (1968), through Matthews (1974), to Bauer et al. (2013). It is no coincidence, in this context, that John Lyons taught me about all this material when I was an undergraduate. Despite this direct descent, there is room for some vagueness and even theoretical disagreement in the model. For instance, if we say that *spoiled* is the past tense of SPOIL in a sentence like (i), and the past participle of SPOIL in a sentence like (ii), do we have a single word-form with two different tokens in (i) and (ii), or do we have two distinct but homophonous° word-forms in (i) and (ii)? Personally, I tend to take the latter view, but can find no evidence to support this view or even to suggest that the distinction is vital.

(i) It spoiled my aim.
(ii) It had spoiled my aim.

Perhaps more centrally, if we take a word like *every* which only has one word-form, can we claim that there is a lexeme EVERY, or do we have lexemes only when there are different word-forms? In other words, is there a lexemic level of representation, where everything is expressed in terms of lexemes? I tend to believe there is a lexeme EVERY, but the point is controversial.

There are other types of word to which I have paid no attention here: phonological words, lexical items made up of several lexemes (*to split up, high horse, to kick the bucket*), and grammatical° (as opposed to lexical°) words. Words that have multiple word-forms tend to be lexical words, words whose meaning makes reference to entities, actions or states in the real world; those with a single form tend to be grammatical words°, words whose function is to signal grammatical relationships. This might be an argument for using the term 'lexeme' only for lexical words, but there are so many exceptions in both directions that such a solution remains awkward. For example, if we accept an adverb like *happily* as a word with one word-form (and not as itself a form of HAPPY), it has lexical semantic content, but no paradigm° of forms to make it a lexeme. Also *be* as an auxiliary (as in *The starling is seen in the countryside*) and *be* as a main verb (as in *The starling is a pest in the countryside*) may have identical paradigms, but the auxiliary might be viewed as a grammatical word and the main verb as a lexical word. Incidentally, the distinction between 'morphosyntactic word' and 'grammatical word' drawn here follows Bauer et al. (2013), although some use the terms interchangeably.

The illustrations in this chapter have been exclusively from English, but the problem of the nature of the word is made all the more difficult if it is viewed cross-linguistically, see Bauer (2000) and Dixon and Aikhenvald (2002).

Reading

Any good introduction to morphology will provide a discussion of lexemes and word-forms. Bauer (2003) and Aronoff and Fudeman (2011) provide quite full discussions. Lyons (1968) provides a relatively early discussion, which has been extremely influential. For a more nuanced, typological, view of word, Dixon and Aikhenvald (2002) is recommended.

Talking about theory brings us straight into the field of science, and, more specifically, the philosophy of science. Many linguists claim that linguistics is a science, but there are some who are less convinced. I suspect that it does not matter much. Whether or not linguistics is a science, it deals with observation, classification, building hypotheses, testing hypotheses and making predictions based on these hypotheses. It is still important to know what phenomena are actually observed (e.g. that *cats* refers to several feline animals), and what phenomena are theoretical constructs, the product of the analyst's mind, and open to discussion (e.g. that there is something called a 'lexeme'). Good introductions to the philosophy of science are Chalmers (1999) and French (2007). These works do not necessarily answer all the questions that a linguist may have, but they provide the philosophical background.

Discussion questions

Some suggested answers to these questions can be found in the Answers to Discussion Questions at edinburghuniversitypress.com/rethinkingmorphology

1. Is the ultimate truth (if we can imagine any such thing) related in any way to how many people believe in a particular theory at a particular time? What does this tell you about theories and about truth?
2. Most of the hypotheses that we choose to believe in or choose not to believe in are ones which we are unable to judge scientifically or where it is not clear what criteria we ought to use to determine how successful a particular hypothesis is. These might be hypotheses such as:

(a) Taking in refugees is good/bad for the receiving country.
(b) Having fewer laws leads to better/worse outcomes for the population of the country with fewer laws.
(c) Being able to speak more than one language is good/bad for the individuals concerned and for the communities in which those individuals live.

Choose one of these hypotheses, and consider the problems it raises. Why is any media sound-bite likely to be inaccurate? What are the implications for hypotheses about linguistic structure?

3. If we know that there are many kinds of word, but we cannot define 'word' in a satisfactory way even for English, let alone for all languages, how useful is it to look at the internal structure of the word (which is what morphology is about)?
4. Why are the two following claims not identical? Can you think of circumstances where one might be true and the other false?

   (a) WALK is an intransitive° verb.
   (b) *Walk* is an intransitive° verb.

5. From the sentence *My films are not comedies, but there's comedy in them* (from David Lynch), list the lexemes, the word-forms, the grammatical words, the lexical words, the morphosyntactic words and the orthographic words.
6. Is the word something that we observe or is it a theoretical construct?

2 Morpheme-based morphology

2.1 A sketch morphemic model

Anyone who has said that *cats* means 'more than one cat' because it's got *cat* in it and an *-s* that means 'plural' (or anything equivalent) has in effect analysed a word in terms of morphemes. So although the notion of morpheme° as a linguistic unit is an invention of the late nineteenth century, the fundamental insight behind the morpheme was not particularly new.

Having said that, there never was, and certainly is not today, a single coherent view held by all theorists of what the morpheme is. There are variants of morpheme theory. In this section, a fundamental morphemic model will be laid out which is something of an amalgam of the models that were available in the first part of the twentieth century. Because the idea of the morpheme was based, often consciously, on the idea of the phoneme°, there was assumed to be a structural analogy° between morphemes and phonemes, and thus between the descriptive theory affecting phonology° and morphology at the period. That structural analogy° will be made overt in this sketch, and leads to a particular approach to the morpheme. Some minor variants will be mentioned in the Notes and comments section at the end of the chapter. The purpose of this sketch is to outline a variant of morpheme theory which can, later in the chapter, be seen to be subject to the various criticisms that have been levelled at morpheme theory in general, without falsifying the record too much.

The morpheme-based approach is best explained by consideration of some relevant examples. As a first example, take the word *empowerments*. A dictionary-like gloss of this word would be something like 'several actions of putting someone or something into a position of power', and we can divide *empowerments* into various elements to which parts of this meaning can be attributed. Perhaps most obviously, and already noted, the final *-s* regularly accompanies the meaning 'more than one', and can be found in other words such as *books*, *cats*, *entertainments*, *envelopes*, *giraffes*, *streets*, and so on. The segment *-ment* can be found in a number of words where it means something like 'action', as in *appointment*, *conferment*, *development*, *dismemberment*, *payment* and the like. While each of these words has a meaning that could be glossed as 'action', some of them also have other readings: *payment*, for example, could be 'a thing which is paid' as in *Payment has been received*, and *development* might be read as 'the state of something which is developed', as in *The development in her talent is much to be admired.* While this plethora of meanings is quite usual, we need not worry about it just here. The element *em-* can be found with the meaning '(put) into' in words like *embark*, *embody*, *empanel*, and the like. And *power* can stand alone with the meaning 'power'. So each of these elements recurs with a particular form accompanied by a particular meaning (perhaps set of meanings). Moreover, the meaning of *empowerments* can be, to a very large extent, calculated from the meanings of these elements. Although there are individual exceptions, in general terms there will be only one way to analyse a word into recurrent meaningful elements of this kind. Thus although *syllable* might look as though it ends in the same element as *employable*, *syllable* does not mean (to parallel the case of *employable*) 'able to be sylled'; although it might look as though *cartridge* could be split into *cart* and *ridge*, *cartridge* is not related in meaning to *cart* or *ridge*, and while *spoonfed* might look (at least in writing) as though it should be the past tense of a verb SPOONF, there is no such verb.

If a word can be exhaustively analysed into elements which also occur in other words, and which are associated with the same meaning in all cases, we term these elements 'morphs°'. So *empowerments* contains the morphs *em-*, *power*, *-ment* and *-s*. There is no remainder. These morphs differ from each other in a number of ways. *Power* can stand as a word on its own and is thus a (potentially) 'free morph°', while the others cannot occur alone, and must be joined onto some other morph before they can make up a word. These are therefore (obligatorily) 'bound morphs°'. *Power* is also the central part of the meaning of this word, the part to which affixes° (prefixes° and suffixes°) are added, and is the 'root°'. The morph *em-* precedes the material to which it is attached, and is a 'prefix°', while *-ment* and *-s* follow the material to which they are attached and are 'suffixes°'. And *-s* creates a word-form of the lexeme EMPOWERMENT, and is 'inflectional°', while the other morphs which are affixes create new lexemes, and are 'derivational°'. All of these are ways of subclassifying morphs.

The morph *-ment* always recurs with precisely the same form. But sometimes we find two (or more) morphs which are phonologically similar to each other, which are synonymous°, which do not occur in the same conditions, and which, between them, cover a full range of possible environments. This is called complementary distribution°. Consider the *-s* at the end of *empowerments.* In a word like this, it is pronounced /s/; in a word like *refusals* the *-s* suffix is pronounced /z/; and in a word like *governesses* we find an element which has the same meaning, but spelt *-es* and pronounced /ɪz/ (in some varieties of English /əz/). These three forms all mean 'plural', they all contain an alveolar fricative and so are deemed phonologically similar, and they are in complementary distribution: the form /ɪz/ occurs following a strident° (any of /s, z, ʃ, ʒ, ʧ, ʤ/) as the last element preceding the suffix; the form /s/ occurs following anything that is not a strident, but is voiceless°; and the form /z/ applies everywhere else – that is, following any non-strident voiced° segment. This distribution is phonologically explicable. English never allows clusters of strident phonemes such as */ss/ or */ʃs/ or */ʤz/, and so any sequence of stridents has to be broken up by a vowel. Everywhere else, voiceless° /s/ follows anything voiceless, and voiced° /z/ follows anything voiced. These morphs are termed 'allomorphs°' of a single 'morpheme°'. The parallel with allophones° of a phoneme° is important here. In the phonological instance, allophones must be phonetically similar to each other ([h] and [ŋ] cannot be allophones of the same phoneme), must be in complementary distribution (or, for some, in free variation°), so that they never contrast, and must have the same function for the speaker (speakers tend to think of them as being the same sound). In the phonological case, we talk about allophones of a phoneme; in the morphological case, we talk about 'allomorphs' of a 'morpheme'. So the morpheme which we can call {z} or {plural} has three allomorphs, /s/, /z/ and /ɪz/. Similarly, the morpheme {en-} has allomorphs *em-* as in *empower, embark* and *en-* as in *enrage, enthrone,* with the <m> preceding a bilabial and the <n> found elsewhere. The morpheme {ment}, however, has only one allomorph, *-ment.* Note the notation for morphemes and allomorphs.

In what follows, we shall consider various difficulties for a model of this kind, and criticisms that have been made of the notion of morpheme as a result.

2.2 Problems for the morpheme

There are innumerable problems for the morpheme and criticisms of it. Some of them are no more than difficulties of analysis, while others are central to the nature of the entity. In each case below, the problem will be explained, and then the case to minimise the impact of the supposed problem will be presented. In every case, these will be headed 'The problem' and 'The defence'. The problems are presented loosely from easiest to most difficult, but the order of presentation is not significant.

2.2.1 *How much similarity of form must allomorphs share?*

The problem

If allomorphs have to be phonologically similar, how similar is similar enough for allomorphy to be established? Consider plural formation in English. We have already seen that there are allomorphs /z/, /s/ and /ɪz/ which are in complementary distribution, but what about the form /ən/ which occurs in *oxen*? Is that another allomorph of {plural}, or is there a new morpheme {en} which also means 'plural'? Both /z/ and /n/ are alveolar consonants and both are voiced. Are these characteristics sufficient to let us say that they are phonologically similar enough to be allomorphs of the same morpheme? In addition, there are nouns in English which have other plural markers (some are shown in (1)), and we can ask whether all of these contain the same morpheme or not.

(1)	alumnus	alumni
	bacterium	bacteria
	basis	bases (/beɪsiːz/)
	cherub	cherubim
	corpus	corpora
	foot	feet
	formula	formulae
	larynx	larynges
	sheep	sheep

To take a different kind of example, do the words *eight*, *octameter* and *octosyllabic* share any morpheme, and if so, what is that morpheme and how much of the form of these words does it make up? The general question here is whether the notion of morpheme is a well-defined one if analysts cannot agree on what are or are not morphemes.

The defence

The more general question here is whether there is any problem with synonymous° morphemes (to match synonymous expressions such as HORSE CHESTNUT and CONKER, CHIROPODIST and PODIATRIST, or FLASH DRIVE and USB STICK). If there is no problem with synonymy in general, then the *-en* in *oxen* and the other forms illustrated in (1) can belong to synonymous morphemes (a range of forms meaning 'plural') rather than to allomorphs of the same morpheme. Although this seems unobjectionable, the analysis provided in most introductory texts is for there to be a single morpheme {plural} to which all of the variants illustrated belong. Such an analysis seems to prioritise similarity of meaning over similarity of form° in allomorphy.

There is another issue to consider here, which may provide an alternative defence. The analysis of /z/, /s/ and /ɪz/ as allomorphs of the same morpheme depended upon the distribution of the allomorphs being phonologically predictable. In the other instances, the distribution of the various plural forms is predictable only in terms of the lexemes° involved (OX takes the plural *-en*, but BOX, COX, FOX take the expected /ɪz/ plural affix): that is, the distribution of the allomorphs is conditioned° by the individual lexemes, and not by the phonology. Furthermore, that lexical conditioning° does not always specify a single possibility: the plural of *octopus* may be *octopusses*, *octopi* or *octopodes*. Phonologically conditioned allomorphs are the more central cases of allomorphy, but the theory does not rule out lexical or other kinds of conditioning for allomorphs.

In the *eight* case, most analysts would probably avoid seeing a shared morpheme – perhaps for reasons which will be discussed in Section 2.2.3. But there is no principled reason why these words could not be analysed as having a morpheme in common.

In general, just as we know that there is almost always a choice of phonemic analyses which will be coherent for a given language (see Chao [1934] 1957), there is no reason to suppose that there is only one justifiable morphemic analysis of a given language, so that disagreements about individual instances should not be problems for the notion of morpheme.

2.2.2 How much similarity of meaning must the allomorphs share?

The problem

If the amount of form allomorphs° must share is sometimes unclear, so is the amount of meaning. Again, two fairly standard examples make the point.

The words *brother*, *father*, *mother* share the form *-ther*, but is that sufficient to establish a morpheme° here? We can perhaps postulate a meaning 'member of the nuclear family', but then why does *sister* not share the form (or is *-ter* an allomorph?), and what about *son* and *daughter*? If we reject this analysis, is it because of the postulated meaning, or is it because the meaning is restricted to so few words?

A much more awkward example is provided by a series of words of English that are borrowed from Latin. Some relevant forms are set out

Table 2.1 Some words containing Latin prefixes borrowed into English

	Latin prefix *con-*	Latin prefix *de-*	Latin prefix *ex-*	Latin prefix *in-*	Latin prefix *re-*
Latin base *duce*	conduce	deduce	educe	induce	reduce
Latin base *fer*	confer	defer		infer	refer
Latin base *mit*	commit	demit	emit		remit
Latin base *port*	comport	deport	export	import	report

in Table 2.1. In order to discuss this case, we need a little more terminology. It is sometimes the case that we are dealing with a piece of form° whose status as a morph (and so representing or realising° a morpheme) is unclear: we may simply not know whether something is a morph or not, we may have an instance where scholars disagree as to whether it is a morpheme, or we may have a case where we are fairly sure that, whatever it is, it is not a morph. In such cases we can use the term 'formative°'. With the examples in Table 2.1, the first formative was a prefix in Latin, but its status in English is controversial.

The question with regard to the words in Table 2.1 is whether the etymological° prefixes or the etymological bases° (the things to which the affixes are attached) have any consistent meaning in English. In other words, are these formatives morphs in English or not? Those who have studied Latin often see similarities in these sets; those who have not studied Latin usually fail to see a relationship. What do *induce* 'to persuade or influence to do something' and *reduce* 'to make something less or smaller' have in common semantically? What does *reduce* have in common with *report* 'to give people information about something'? (Definitions from Hornby 2000.)

However, the etymological bases, at least, do show some consistent behaviour in English. All these words ending in *-mit* have nominalisations° in *-mission*; all the words ending in *-duce* have nominalisations in *-duction*. What is more, these nominalisations are unpredictable except in terms of the etymological base. The verbs *vomit* and *spruce (up)*, which do not have the relevant etymology, do not have nominalisations **vomission* and **spruction*.

To set up a morpheme on the basis of this patterned way of making nominalisations, however, is to give form precedence over meaning in the form–meaning relationship that defines the morpheme in our model.

The question is whether we are justified in recognising a morpheme if there is similarity in form°, but no similarity in meaning.

The defence

It is clear that there is a relationship between *emit* and *emission* and that this relationship is based on the formative° *mit*. But the relationship between *-mit* and *-mission* is a fact about the morphology of Latin, which English has simply borrowed. This does not imply that *mit* is a morpheme° in English. With *brother*, *father*, *mother*, if there ever was a morphological relationship, it goes back to Indo-European. In either case, the relationship in modern English is purely coincidental and not morphological. Not every relationship of form is necessarily morphological. *Mangos* are not related to *mangosteens*, and neither is a *goose* related to a *mongoose*: the formal relationships are purely coincidental, and the same is true of *brother*, *father* and *mother*.

2.2.3 What are the limits of analysis?

The problem

In the last two sections we have seen instances where it is not clear whether we can analyse something into morphs or not. Is there any way we can determine whether *brother*, *father* and *mother* can be analysed morphologically, and so on? It is clear that different analysts draw the line in different places. A nice example is provided by names of instruments that end in *-er*. Nouns like *amplifier*, *blender*, *recliner*, *revolver* and *sparkler* denote instruments: an amplifier is an instrument (or a thing – but specifically not a person) which amplifies, and so on. The words *barrier*, *dagger*, *hammer*, *tether*, *trencher*, *trigger* and others also denote instruments, but they are not based on current verbs: a hammer is not, in current standard English, a thing which hams. Do we analyse the *-er* in *hammer* as the same *-er* that we find in *revolver*, or not? If we do not, is there any relationship between *hammer* and *revolver*?

The defence

Although there are some authorities who treat the *-er* forms in *hammer* and *revolver* as the same (Bloomfield [1933] 1935, for instance), there is an argument for not doing so. It is part of the definition of morphs° that they must exhaustively analyse° a word. Thus, if we analyse an *-er* morph in *hammer*, we must also analyse a *hamm-* morph. But the only evidence we have for there being a *hamm-* morph is the word *hammer*. This morph is not recurrent. It is a 'unique morph°'. While there are places where analysts feel obliged to analyse unique morphs, any analysis which creates large numbers of unique morphs must be subject to intense scrutiny. In the case of *brother*, *father* and *mother*, the price for analysing *-ther* as a morph would be the creation of three unique morphs *bro-*, *fa-* and *mo-*, and so this analysis is highly suspect.

Against such a background, we have to consider words like *hatred* and *bishopric*. Here again we have the option of analysing unique morphs *-red* and *-ric*, but this time, if we do so we do not create any other unique morphs: *hate* and *bishop* already exist. Moreover, although we do not find other words which have the suffixes *-red* and *-ric*, these words do fit into sets of suffixed words. The suffix° in *hat-red* is like the suffixes in *admir-ation*, *depart-ure*, *encourage-ment*, *grow-th*, and so on in creating a noun from a verb. The suffix in *bishop-ric* is like the suffixes in *count-y*, *king-dom*, *parson-age* and others in creating the name of a domain from the name of a person. These parallels and the low number of such unique morphs seem to lead to their acceptance.

2.2.4 *Empty morphs*

The problem

An 'empty morph°' is a morph which has form but no meaning. This is in direct contravention of the principle outlined above that a morph is a unit which has both constant form and constant meaning. Empty morphs are thus a problem.

Perhaps the most frequent example of empty morphs cited in the literature is the case of so-called 'thematic vowels°' in Latin and Romance. These are illustrated in (2), using data from Italian (Maiden and Robustelli 2000).

(2)

	present	*past*	*imperfect*
'sing			
1st singular	canto	cantai	cantavo
1st plural	cantiamo	cantammo	cantavamo
'fear'			
1st singular	temo	temei	temevo
1st plural	temiamo	tememmo	temevamo
'sleep'			
1st singular	dormo	dormii	dormivo
1st plural	dormiamo	dormimmo	dormivamo

In (2) the verb stems° (that part of the verb to which inflectional affixes are added) are *cant-*, *tem-* and *dorm-* respectively, and the first person singular ending in the present and the imperfect is *-o*. In the past, it is *-i*. The 1st plural ending is *-(a)mo*. The imperfect marker is *-v*.

However, this does not account for the entire word-form: the *-i* in the 1st plural of the present tense is probably part of the allomorph of the 1st plural marker found in the present tense. The extra *-m* in the past tense could have the same analysis. Nothing hinges on this for the present case. However, in the past tense form we have an unexplained *-a*, *-e* or *-i* before the person ending, and the same vowel occurs before the imperfect marker. This is the thematic vowel°. Since the meaning 'first person singular of the imperfect of CANTARE/TEMERE/DORMIRE' is covered by the other morphs we have considered, it appears that this vowel has no meaning. If we assume, as we have, that there must be no remainder when a word is analysed into morphs, the vowel must be a morph. It is an empty morph because it carries no meaning.

The defence

There are at least two possible defences here. The first is that an analysis where these vowels are separate morphs is not necessary: we could have three allomorphs of the imperfect marker: *-av*, *-ev* and *-iv*. Perhaps more likely, we could have two allomorphs of each stem, one without the vowel and one with. We would need a similar analysis for the past tense instances. It is true that such an analysis is messy, not maximally economical, and that the conditioning° factor for each of the allomorphs would not be phonological (see the comments in Section 2.2.1). Nonetheless, to say that there is a possible analysis of these forms where we need an empty morph is rather different from saying that the only possible analysis of these forms requires an empty morph.

The second defence is that the morph does have meaning, or at least, it has a function, which may be the same thing. Its function is to show which conjugation° of Italian verbs the individual verb belongs to. The meaning of the *-a* is, if you like, 'A-conjugation class'.

Although it is not possible to say that there are no examples of empty morphs which cannot be rebutted in one of these ways, these defences certainly seem to work most of the time, if not all the time.

2.2.5 Zero morphs

The problem

If it is a problem to find a form with no meaning (Section 2.2.4), it is an equivalent problem to find a meaning with no form°. There is general agreement that we must not set up a morpheme whose only realisations are zeroes (this is sometimes called the 'overt analogue criterion°'), but not everyone agrees about morphemes which are – apparently, at least – sometimes not marked. So nobody suggests setting up a morpheme {imperative} in English, because the imperative form of the verb in English (as in *leave!*, *stand!*) does not have any morph marking it. Rather we say that the imperative is unmarked° in English, and there is a great deal of evidence that what is unmarked across languages tends to be predictable from general principles (though there are exceptions to the general rule).

We will consider two rather different cases where it has been claimed that there is meaning without form, and where it has been proposed that there should be a 'zero morph°' (a morph of no form) included in the analysis. Note that since a morph is defined as a form, a form with no form is an embarrassment.

In the first example, linguists refer to sets of data such as that in (3).

(3)	black	blacken
	equal	equalise
	false	falsify
	rich	enrich
	empty	empty

In the first four examples in (3), a verb meaning, more or less, 'to cause to be ~' is created by adding an affix° to an adjective. In the last example, however, no affix appears. The parallels suggest that there should be an affix with the meaning 'causative', so in the case of *empty*, we should add an affix, call it Ø (zero), to match the other cases, and to explain the transformation from adjective to causative verb. Since there are many parallel cases to this in English, the use of such a zero morph turns out to be widespread once this analysis is accepted.

The second case is rather less general, and can be illustrated from some Russian paradigms°. Some partial paradigms are set out in (4) (Ward 1965).

(4)	*'table', masculine noun*		*'word', neuter noun*	
	singular	*plural*	*singular*	*plural*
nominative	stol	stolý	slóvo	slová
genitive	stolá	stolóv	slóva	slov
dative	stolú	stolám	slóvu	slovám
instrumental	stolóm	stolámi	slóvom	slovámi

Here, the masculine nominative° singular has no suffix, but this is not surprising: this is one of the cases where the lack of marking is widespread across languages, as mentioned above. But the general expectation is that other cases° will be marked in a language that shows morphological case°. In particular, the more complex the combination of number and case, the more likely there is to be an overt affix.

Cross-linguistically, there is no reason to expect the genitive° plural to be unmarked, which is what we see in the Russian data. To gain the expected generalisation that all cases except the nominative singular will be marked (and even then, the nominative singular of some nouns is marked), we can say that there is a zero-suffix marking the genitive plural for *slóvo* and words like it.

The defence

The first of these cases is rather easier to rebut than the second. First, we have to note that given that we have a prefix as well as suffixes with the causative meaning illustrated in (3), in principle we cannot tell whether the zero would be a prefix or a suffix. This is a minor irritant, but nevertheless a theoretical problem. More seriously, if we have an zero-morph on the verb *emptyØ*$]_V$ (i.e. on the verb made up of *empty* and a zero suffix), we presumably also have a zero morph on the noun *emptyØ*$]_N$ (as in *He threw away the empty*). So we have two different zeroes, which contrast with each other, and which contrast with *empty*$]_A$ which has no zero. While this is bad enough, the form *round* can be a preposition, adverb, adjective, noun or verb, and we would have to deal with a plethora of contrasting zeroes, as well as with determining which one of these has no zero. At the very least this is psycholinguistically difficult to justify. The analysis of these words with or without a zero remains controversial: those who use a zero talk about 'zero-derivation°', and those who do not use a zero talk about 'conversion°' in these cases.

In the Russian instance, we know that the zero must be a suffix, and the occurrence is much more restricted, without any proliferation of zeroes. In this case, arguments against the zero are much weaker, but we can still raise questions about its necessity and about its psycholinguistic reality: it is not clear why we need to postulate an affix where there is none in the superficial data we are presented with if it is just to make the analysis look more consistent with cross-linguistic patterns.

2.2.6 Processes as morphs

The problem

Consider the pairs of words in (5), which are related nouns and verbs. English shows similar formal relationships between adjectives and verbs and in singular and plural nouns.

(5)	*noun*	*verb*
	belief	believe
	house /haʊs/	house /haʊz/

mouth /maʊθ/	mouth /maʊð/
strife	strive
wreath	wreathe

A similar case is provided by the strong verbs of English and other Germanic languages. Consider the pairs in (6).

(6)	*stem form*	*past tense*
	bleed	bled
	rise	rose
	run	ran
	see	saw
	swim	swam
	swing	swung

And finally, consider the examples from French in (7), where the difference between the masculine and feminine forms of a class of adjectives is presented. The data is presented in transcription, since the spelling masks the phonological relationship.

(7)	*gloss*	*masculine*	*feminine*
	'big'	gʀã	gʀãd
	'fat'	gʀo	gʀos
	'happy'	øʀø	øʀøz
	'honest'	fʀã	fʀãʃ
	'small'	pti	ptit

In (5) there is no suffix, but the final fricative changes its voicing. In (6) one vowel is replaced by another vowel. In (7) we see that the difference between the masculine and feminine form of the adjective lies in the final consonant, but that consonant is variable, and cannot be predicted from the masculine form of the adjective. The standard solution to the problem is that there is a case of subtraction° here: if we take the feminine form as the basic form of the adjective, we can regularly derive the masculine form by taking off the final consonant.

What these three cases have in common is that there appears to be some kind of process that links the relevant forms. In (5) the process is one of voicing (or, possibly, devoicing) of the final fricative; in (6) the process is of replacing one vowel with another; in (7) the process is removing a consonant. In the literature, it is sometimes said that what we have here is a 'replacive morph°', which we might write as f → v, i → a, ʃ → Ø, and so on. But these are processes, not forms, and a morph is defined as a form. They are thus an embarrassment to morphemic theory.

The defence

The simplest way out of the problem is simply to say that *belief* and *believe*, *swim* and *swam*, *petit* /pti/ and *petite* /ptit/ are different morphs, and to deny any process linking them. This is not particularly satisfactory in the light of the data (although in (5) and (7) the historical processes which gave rise to the patterns illustrated are very different from the synchronic° processes which now appear to relate the forms), but it solves a problem for the theory. There is a long history of positing various closely related morphs (often representing the same lexeme, as in (6) and (7)): Russian verbs may have several stems° with different vowels in them (Ward 1965: 117), and in Latin a suppletive° supine° form (i.e. one whose form is not related to the form of the root of the verb) such as *lātum* from *ferō* 'to bear' gives rise to words such as *lātor* 'mover of a motion', *lātūra* 'carrying of burdens' and so becomes a base° in other derivations° as well as in the inflectional° system. Multiple morphs representing the same morpheme are in themselves, therefore, not problematic.

2.2.7 Cumulative exponence

The problem

If we go back to the Russian data in (4) and look for a piece of form° that shows that a noun is plural, we will be unsuccessful. There is nothing in the plural forms which recurs only in the plural (indeed, the genitive° singular of the word for 'table' shows the same affix as the nominative° plural of the word for 'word'). Neither is there anything which consistently marks the nominative° case,° or any of the other cases. Since there are also feminine nouns in Russian which have a different pattern again, and there are more cases in Russian than were illustrated in (4), the problem is more difficult than is obvious from (4). If the morpheme demands association of meaning with form and we find a meaning without any associated form, then we cannot postulate a morpheme here. This phenomenon is called 'cumulative exponence°' because the formal elements act as exponents° or realisations° of several meaning elements at once.

The defence

The argument assumes that every piece of meaning must have its own piece of form, and vice versa. This is sometimes called biuniqueness°. By that argument, we have to say that the -s on the end of *prefers* is the exponent of three independent meanings: 'third person', 'singular' and 'present tense'. But the suffix *-s* is found only when these three occur together (except in the irregular verb BE). It would seem more economical to say that the meaning of this *-s* is 'third person singular of the present tense' – one piece of form, one meaning. The Russian case is more complex, but the fundamental principle is the same. We have to recognise a number of affixes which mean things like 'instrumental singular of a masculine noun'. Again, this may not be the maximally economical way to specify forms corresponding to syntactic information, because several forms corresponding to a meaning like 'instrumental' will have to be given. Nevertheless, it provides a perfectly coherent morphological analysis.

2.2.8 *Extended exponence*

The problem

Consider the examples in (8), which illustrate the singular and plural second person forms of the Latin verb AMO 'I love' in four tenses: the present, the perfect, the pluperfect and the future perfect (Kennedy 1962). The data set is simplified by illustrating only one conjugation class, only some of the tenses°, and only the indicative° (and not the subjunctive°).

(8) amās 'you (SG) love'
amātis 'you (PL) love'
amāvistī 'you (SG) have loved'
amāvistis 'you (PL) have loved'
amāverās 'you (SG) had loved'
amāverātis 'you (PL) had loved'
amāveris 'you (SG) will have loved'
amāveritis 'you (PL) will have loved'

In the data in (8) we can make the following linkages between form and meaning:

i. *am-* is the root representing the lexeme° AMO 'I love'
ii. *-ā* is the thematic vowel° (see Section 2.2.4)
iii. *-s* marks the second person singular in the present, the pluperfect and the future perfect, but not in the perfect.
iv. *-tis* marks the second person plural
v. the present tense is unmarked, that is, there is no morph° which specifically shows this tense
vi. *-v* is the perfect marker°, present in all perfect tenses
vii. *-er* is present in the pluperfect and the future perfect; we might take it to indicate a time-'shifted' perfect, but as it is only present in the perfect tenses, it also marks perfect
viii. *-i* is found in the perfect and the future perfect, but not in the pluperfect, and so marks 'non-past perfect'
ix. *-ā* is found only in the pluperfect

x. *-s* is found only in the perfect
xi. *-tī* marks second person singular only in the perfect.

Thus, in the word-form *amāvistī* we find the relationships indicated in (9).

(9)

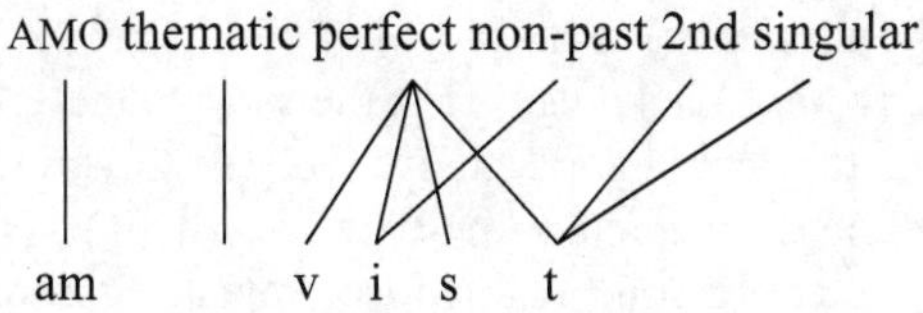

The point to note with the representation in (9) is that perfect is realised° by four separate morphs, some of which also represent something else (further cases of cumulative exponence°, see Section 2.2.7). When we find the same meaning represented by multiple pieces of form (sometimes not even contiguous pieces of form), we speak of 'extended exponence'. The problem for morpheme theory is that there is no single piece of form corresponding to the relevant meaning, but the meaning is spread over several forms, but the notion of morpheme is based on the idea that there is a link between one form and one meaning.

The defence

The only way to return to a biunique° situation where each form has a meaning and each meaning has a form here is to treat *-vistī* in (9) as a single morph. This solves the question of extended exponence, but increases the number of morphs (and hence morphemes°) in the grammar and is not particularly economical. It is not economical because it will also be necessary to recognise meanings such as 'non-past', 'second person' or 'singular' separately or in other combinations in other parts of the grammar.

2.2.9 Superfluous morphs

The problem

Consider the data from Italian in (10) (Maiden and Robustelli 2000). Here the adverb has as its base° something which looks just like the feminine form of the adjective. This happens whether the feminine form is specifically marked as such (by having an *-a* morph on the end) or not (as in *cortese*, where the masculine and feminine forms of the adjective are identical).

(10)

	masculine	*feminine*	*adverb*	
'blind'	cieco	cieca	ciecamente	'blindly'
'next'	prossimo	prossima	prossimamente	'shortly'

'painful'	dolorso	dolorosa	dolorosamente	'painfully'
'polite'	cortese	cortese	cortesemente	'politely'
'serious'	serio	seria	seriamente	'seriously'

The difficulty here is that although the feminine form of the adjective is used as a base°, and there appears to be a specific morph to mark that status in many instances, there is no meaning 'feminine' involved in the meaning of the adverbs. This means that the morpheme° {feminine} cannot be part of the morphemic analysis of the adverbs: it is inappropriate or superfluous in the make-up of the adverb forms. There is a well-known etymological reason for this form appearing here, but we are not dealing with the etymology° of these words, but with their morphology, and it is problematical.

The defence

There are various possible counterarguments to the position outlined above, but none of them is entirely satisfactory. Where the feminine form of the adjective ends in *-a* (as is most often the case), we might claim that there is a homophonous° but not synonymous° *-a* (and so a different morpheme) that occurs in the adverbial form. We might, alternatively, claim that the suffix forming adverbs is *-amente*, and that there is an allomorph *-mente* which occurs when the affix is attached to a full word rather than something shorter than a full word. We might, following the argument from French adjectives in (7) (and French has data parallel to the Italian data discussed here) suggest that the feminine form of the adjective is the fundamental form, the default form – but there is little to support that notion in Italian, and even in French it might be difficult to extend the argument beyond the class illustrated in (7). We could claim that we have an empty morph° here, and solve it as we have solved other questions of empty morphs (see Section 2.2.4), but that is to lose a generalisation that whatever the feminine form of the adjective is, whether it is homophonous° with the masculine or specifically marked as feminine, that is what occurs before *-mente*. In other words, although we can find ways to force an alternative analysis, none is very satisfactory.

2.2.10 Morphs with incompatible meanings

The problem

The examples in (11) are taken from the Latin verbal system, and illustrate the first person singular of various tenses of verbs in two conjugations (Kennedy 1962).

(11) amō 'I love'
amābō 'I shall love'
amābam 'I was loving'
amāvī 'I have loved'
amāveram 'I had loved'

moneō 'I advise'
monēbō 'I shall advise'
monēbam 'I was advising'
monuī 'I have advised'
monueram 'I had advised'

We can find the root of the verb easily, and the thematic vowel° (see Section 2.2.4). The <u> and the <v> (pronounced [w]) are allomorphs depending on the phonetic environment, and mark the perfect. There are various first person singular markers°, depending on the tense°. But what does the *-b* mark? It arises in the future and in the imperfect, but it is not clear that these two tenses have anything semantic in common that is not shared by other tenses. In other words, this *-b* seems to be a form associated with two distinct and contrasting meanings: 'future' and 'imperfect'.

The defence

If we consider, rather than Latin, the English morphological system, we find an <s> (/z/) on the end of words like *bananas* (where it means 'plural') and *prefers* (where it means, among other things, 'singular'). In this instance, nobody suggests that the two -s affixes must realise° the same morpheme because of their common form; rather we say we have two homophonous° but non-synonymous morphs which, because of their meaning, realise° different morphemes. If we now return to the Latin, we can have the same solution: just because we have a form *-b* occurring in two places in the paradigm, there is no reason to suppose that it must represent the same morpheme on both occasions. There can be no objection to having different but homophonous morphs with distinct meanings, and saying that the *-b-* in *amābō* realises the morpheme {future}, while the one in *amābam* realises {imperfect}.

2.2.11 Inversion

The problem

The examples in (12) are from Plains Cree (Klaiman 1992). The gloss DIR means 'direct' and INV means 'inverse'. The words are divided into morphs for ease of comprehension.

(12) (a)

Ni-	pēh	-ā	-nān	-ak
1st	wait	DIR	1PL	3PL

'We await them'

(b)

Ni-	pēh	-iko	-nān	-ak
1st	wait	INV	1PL	3PL

'They await us'

The problem is that the marker for the first person plural in (12a) shows the subject of the sentence, while in (12b), although identical in both form and position to what we find in (12a), it shows the direct object of the sentence. The marker meaning '3PL' has just the opposite readings. If the same form in the same position has two diametrically opposed meanings, how can we have forms and meanings related directly to each other?

The defence

There are two main arguments to provide a solution to this problem. The first is that the two occurrences of *-nān* and *-ak* are not in the same environment. They are in different environments because of the direct and inverse markers which precede them. In the terminology established by Chomsky (1964) for phonology, this is a case of 'local determinacy°'. And just as it was accepted by many phonemicists that if the environment told you which phoneme a particular phone belonged to, there was no problem for phoneme theory, so if the environment tells you which morpheme a particular morph belongs to, there is no problem for morpheme theory.

This argument is fine as long as direct and inverse are, indeed, marked in the relevant forms (or at least, as long as one of them is). Unfortunately, it is not always the case in all languages that show inversion that the status is marked overtly. Then we have to seek another explanation.

Such an alternative explanation comes in the meaning assigned to the person-markers. The description above assumed that the person markers were identifying subject and object. But in languages which show inversion, the person markers typically reflect the hierarchy of entities involved in the action. First and second persons typically outrank third persons, humans outrank animals, and so on. Such a hierarchy is generally known as an 'animacy hierarchy°', and is important in a number of languages in rather different ways. So in a language with inversion, the markers show relative position on the hierarchy, and since first person outranks third person, first person precedes third person in both (12a) and (12b). Whether the first or third person is the subject of the verb or not is not shown overtly by the inverse marker, and may have to be deduced from contextual clues; crucially, it is not part of the meaning of the morphemes, and that being the case, there is no problem with inverse languages as far as the morpheme is concerned.

2.3 Evaluation

The list of problems for the morpheme given here has not been exhaustive, but the discussion has given a good picture of the kinds of problems that have been brought up in the literature. I think it is probably fair to say that no one of these problems would individually be sufficient to call the notion of the morpheme into question. But there is not just one problem: there is a host of problems. The sheer weight of the problems carries its own message. The morpheme cannot escape scot free from such a sustained attack.

It was noted earlier that the model of morpheme theory that was set up at the beginning of this chapter is only one possible theory about the nature of the morpheme anyway. Although no attempt has been made here to set out multiple views of the morpheme (for which see Mugdan 1986), the very fact that scholars cannot agree on the nature of the morpheme is also a weakness: it might be expected that there would be agreement about the nature of one of the fundamental building blocks of language.

For these reasons, morphemes in their classical form are rarely used today, especially not in discussions of inflections (about which we will have more to say in Chapter 3). In some ways this is a loss: without the notion of a morpheme, it is not clear how or whether we can associate meaning with particular parts of the word, not how or whether we can capture the insights provided by the notion of allomorphy. If we consider the alternation that is shown between the words *electric* (with a final /k/) and *electricity* (with /s/ before *-ity*), we can at least describe the alternation in a morphemic model because /k/ alternates with /s/ immediately before certain affixes (this is called 'velar softening°'). If we have no morphemes, and affixes are morphemes, we have no affixes in the same sense, and we have only phonological strings to act as conditioning° factors.

The real problem with the morpheme, as has already been mentioned more than once (e.g. in Sections 2.2.7 and 2.2.8), is that it is not maximally economical. The morpheme is more compatible with a theory of language that does not demand economy of description than with a theory of language in which economy is a major desideratum. The notion of economical description was important in linguistics in the 1940s and 1950s, but became much more so with the introduction of generative theory in the late 1950s and 1960s. Today, with a trend towards more cognitively based theories of language, the demand for economy of description seems less pressing. One of the differences between the human brain and a computer may well be that the human brain does not object to storing a word and also computing what the form of the word will be, and having, as a result, redundant pathways to a single answer. In such an intellectual environment, the notion of morpheme may appear less awkward than has been the case for many years. At the same time, the new cognitive bias may do away with the need for a morpheme altogether, as will be seen in later chapters.

2.4 An alternative?

Although many scholars have given priority to the meaning side of the sign, leaving the formal side to fend for itself, there is an important recent development which focuses on the formal side, and gives much less importance to semantics. If we start with material such as that in Table 2.1, we see that there can be formal patterns which have no corresponding semantic correlates. We can find examples which take this further.

Maiden (2011) discusses at length the changes affecting Latin verbal forms in the Romance languages. An early phonological change meant that the first person singular of the present indicative and the whole of the present subjunctive had one stem° form, while the rest of the present indicative had a different pattern. Maiden calls this the L-pattern, and he illustrates it with the Portuguese forms in (13), where <nh> represents [ɲ].

(13)

tenho 'I have'	tens	tem	temos	tendes	têm
tenha	tenha	tenha	tenhamos	tenhais	tenham

There is nothing semantic to link precisely the first person singular of the present indicative° with all of the present subjunctive°, but the forms not only persist, but the pattern expands between Latin and modern Romance, even where there is no historical justification for it. For example, the Portuguese forms of the verb 'to be able' are presented in (14), where the general distribution of the stems matches the L-pattern of (13), but does not match the pattern of Latin.

(14)

posso 'I can'	podes	pode	podemos	podeis	podem
possa	possas	possa	possamos	possais	possam

The conclusion is that the forms do not represent a particular meaning, but that the pattern of forms nevertheless has a reality independent of meaning. The formal units like *poss-* isolated here are called 'morphomes°'. Their formal patterning is predictable independent of any meaning that may be attached to them.

If we return to the superfluous morphs discussed in Section 2.2.9, we find another place where the morphome may be useful. As was illustrated in (10), the feminine form of the adjective can have a range of different forms. Precisely the same range of forms occurs in the adverb formations, but without any meaning 'feminine'. This is precisely what we would expect with the morphome: a fixed set of forms with predictable occurrence, but no single, invariable meaning.

Notes and comments

It was noted in the chapter that there are various versions of morpheme theory, and only one is presented above. One alternative is that each of the elements we have here called 'morphs' is termed a 'morpheme', and that the grammar consists of a number of rules saying where each of these 'morphemes' can occur. Such a version of a morphemic theory is called (following Hockett [1954] 1957) an Item and Arrangement model (IA for short). In an IA version of the English noun plural, we would note three 'morphemes' /s/, /z/ and /ɪz/, the last occurring only after stridents°, the first occurring only after other voiceless° consonants, and the /z/ occurring elsewhere°: that is, we would have to specify where they occur or their arrangement. In any case we have to note that *-ment*, for instance, occurs after verbs, so this kind of information is always necessary. The version given in the chapter provides a closer parallel with theories of the phoneme°.

The complementary distribution of *em-* and *en-* mentioned in the text could be analysed more closely in phonetic terms (orthographic representations were used in the chapter). In *encode* we often hear [ŋ], in *enforce* a [ɱ], in *enthrone* a dental [n̪], and this is really an extension of the same pattern. The pattern is rather spoilt, however, by the word *enmesh*, which we would expect to be *emmesh* (a spelling which is also found, though rather less commonly).

The general notion of complementary distribution° is not always clear. For some authorities, allophones° (and thus also allomorphs°, presumably) can be in free variation° with each other. That is, you might hear one or the other, but they do not lead to contrasts in meaning. Aspirated or unaspirated /p/ in *Stop!* may be in free variation.

The markers of the plural in *celli* and *cellos* might be in free variation in that word. Both complementary distribution and free variation are ways of describing audible differences which do not affect meaning (do not contrast). For some authors *complementary distribution* is a label which covers both, for others, the two phenomena are distinct, and allophones (and, by extension, allomorphs) are always in complementary distribution.

In relation to the verb-forms in (6), it might be asked why we do not analyse an infixed° vowel (i.e. a morph° inserted into the middle of the root°) in these words indicating the tense. Occasional writers do just that, but it is not a preferred analysis. First, English does not otherwise use infixes, and in general shows 'word-based morphology', where affixes are added to free morphs°. Second, the supposed stem under such an analysis (*sw–m* for *swim*, for instance) never occurs without a vowel in precisely the marked position (which makes this different from what we find in Semitic, for instance). Corresponding to this, a putative *swm* is simply meaningless to English speakers, and, indeed, an impossible form. Similarly, with the *belief* set of words, we do not analyse a suffix *-f*, because *belie* never occurs (with the relevant pronunciation and meaning) in isolation, and because in *belief-system*, *believable*, and so on we always get either the noun or the verb, never just the putative stem. Finally, if we take the infix analysis, then the verb DRAG would have to have a stem *dr–g*, into which we could insert <a> for the present and <u> for the past tense and past participles in those varieties that use that form. But in other varieties, the past tense and past participle are *dragged*, and in some varieties there may be alternation between these forms. But if the stem is *dr–g*, there is no way to get the vowel <a> in *dragged*: *dragged* presupposes a base *drag*. The co-existence of the two seems to suggest that we need a full form *drag* and not simply the consonantal skeleton *dr–g*.

On the overt analogue criterion°, see Sanders (1988). The zero-derivation° analysis of forms like *empty*Ø]$_V$ have been argued to provide counter-evidence to the overt analogue criterion (Sanders 1988; Plag 1999: 223–4), but we can equally argue that if we want to hold on to the overt analogue criterion, we cannot have a zero-derivation analysis of the verb *empty*, but must have some other kind of explanation of such forms. Although the label 'conversion°' does not provide such an explanation, it at least allows for an alternative. Various writers in cognitive grammar have suggested that conversion should be seen as a type of metonymy (e.g. Dirven 1999).

The analysis of the French adjectives in (7) as an instance of subtraction° is controversial. While this seems to be the most economical analysis, it is not necessarily the psychologically real analysis. Indeed, many of the cases that can be analysed as instances of subtraction tend to be treated as cases of addition, if possible. Consider the instances in (i) from Danish:

(i)	biolog	'biologist'	biologi	'biology'
	fysiolog	'physiologist'	fysiologi	'physiology'
	genealog	'genealogist'	genealogi	'genealogy'
	geolog	'geologist'	geologi	'geology'
	psycholog	'psychologist'	psychologi	'psychology'

Although it seems clear that semantically a psychologist is 'a person who (professionally) does psychology' rather than psychology being 'the area of interest of a psychologist', and so the semantic dependency is that the name of the person depends on the name of the subject area, this would probably not be viewed as subtraction, but as affixation of *-i* for the subject matter. Similar examples are available in many European languages.

A rather more robust example of subtraction comes from Koasati. In Koasati, verbs are marked for whether they take a singular or plural object. Some examples (from Kimball 1991: 317–20) are given in (ii). Adjacent identical vowels are pronounced long. Note that /l/ assimilates to an immediately preceding sonorant consonant.

(ii)	*singular*	*plural*	*gloss*
	ataká-a-li-n	aták-li-n	'to hang something'
	albití-i-li-n	albít-li-n	'to place on top of'
	apołó-o-ka-n	apół-ka-n	'to sleep with someone'
	tipá-s-li-n	típ-li-n	'to pick something off'
	simá-t-li-n	sím-mi-n	'to cut up tanned skin'
	tiwá-p-li-n	tíw-wi-n	'to open something'
	łomá-p-li-n	łom-mi-n	'to whip something'
	tałá-f-ka-n	táł-ka-n	'to whittle something'
	tafilá-m-mi-n	tafíl-li-n	'to overturn something'

Note that the form of the singular is not predictable from the form of the plural, so that the singular base must be learnt. The plural form, though, is predictable from the form of the singular: remove all but the initial consonant(s) of the final syllable of the base to create the base for the plural form. This works whether what is removed is a long vowel or a sequence of VC.

On inverse languages, see Klaiman (1992). They are far more diverse than has been indicated here, and interesting for more reasons than just the morphological.

Reading

On the notion of morpheme, see any introduction to morphology or even to linguistics in general. See also Anderson (2015), Bauer (2017a). For some of the original work in this area, see Bloomfield ([1933] 1935), Nida (1949), Hockett ([1954] 1957). For various versions of the morpheme, see Mugdan (1986).

On arguments against the morpheme in general, see in particular Matthews (1972) and Anderson (1992), but also Anderson (2015), Bauer (2017a).

On the morphome, the original work is Aronoff (1994), but the notion has been developed a great deal in the work of Maiden and his colleagues, to which Maiden (2011) provides a readily accessible introduction. For more detailed and complex discussion, see, for example, Cruschina et al. (2013).

Discussion questions

Some suggested answers to these questions can be found in the Answers to Discussion Questions at edinburghuniversitypress.com/rethinkingmorphology

1. In each of the exercises below, the task is to determine what the morphemes are in the data and (where relevant) what the allomorphs are and how they are distributed. Typically, there is more than one solution, so that part of the point of the exercise is to consider alternative solutions, and determine which (if any) is preferable and why.

   (a) brother, father, mother, sister
   (b) recount, recover, refine, reform, resign
   (c) receive, redeem, reflect, regret
   (d) reboot, recycle, re-enter, refresh, reimport
   (e) that, the, them, this, those
   (f) hither, hence, here
   (g) blackbuck, blackguard, blackmail, blacksmith
   (h) Churchilliana, cricketana, gymkhana, railwayana, Victoriana
   (i) disillusion, dislodge, displease, distress, disturb
   (j) dictatorial, doctoral, presidential, structural, suicidal, torrential
   (k) poem, poet; devil, evil

   Factors you may need to consider include:

   i. Is form constant or predictable?
   ii. Is the meaning fixed?

iii. Does the assumed morpheme have any psychological reality for the speaker? Should it have?
iv. What evidence do you have of recurrence?
v. How many unique morphs are created by an analysis into morphs?

2. Consider the data from Basque and Swahili provided below. Divide the words into morphs. Make a list of all the morphs with their form and their meaning. What strategies do you use for determining the forms and the meanings of the morphs? Does this have any implications for the nature of the morpheme?

Basque

nator	'I come'
dator	'she comes'
natorkizu	'I come to you.sg'
datoz	'they come'
gatozkizu	'we come to you.sg'
dakarzu	'you.sg bring her'
datozkigu	'they come to us'
dakarkiguzu	'you.sg bring her to us'
nakarzu	'you.sg bring me'
dakargu	'we bring her'

Note: In Basque, transitive and intransitive verbs take different subject marking (Basque is an 'ergative' language).

Swahili

nilitaka	'I wanted'
walitaka	'they wanted'
watataka	'they will want'
nisasoma	'I am reading'
wasafika	'they are arriving'
nisaandika	'I am writing'
wataimba	'they will sing'

3. Consider the marking of singular and plural in nouns in the languages set out below.

English	
singular	*plural*
dog	dogs
kitchen	kitchens

shoe	shoes	
tiger	tigers	
van	vans	
Finnish		
singular	*plural*	*gloss*
auto	autot	'car'
hylly	hyllyt	'shelf'
pullo	pullot	'bottle'
talo	talot	'house'
Italian		
singular	*plural*	*gloss*
amico	amici	'friend'
fratello	fratelli	'brother'
libro	libri	'book'
zio	zii	'uncle'
Malayalam		
singular	*plural*	*gloss*
puruʂan	puruʂanmaar	'man'
amma	ammamaar	'mother'
sahoodaran	sahoodaranmaar	'brother'
sahoodari	sahoodarimaar	'sister'
Zulu		
singular	*plural*	*gloss*
umfana	abafana	'boy'
umfazi	abafazi	'wife'
umngane	abangane	'friend'
umntwana	abantwana	'child'
umzala	abazala	'cousin'

The languages in this set fall into two groups: those that have one morph° marking the singular and another marking the plural, and those that have only a morph marking the plural. Would you expect to find a language which had a morph marking the plural but no morph marking the singular? Why (not)? Given that a morph requires a form°, and we can never set up a morpheme whose only morphs have zero form (the overt analogue criterion°), do languages which mark only the plural provide a problem for the notion of the morpheme? Why (not)?

If you want to read something about such matters, consult works on Natural Morphology, including Mayerthaler (1981), or an English summary such as that in Bauer (2003) or the papers in Dressler et al. (1987).

4. Consider the data from English below, which is presented in transcription to allow identity of form to be visible. We have two morphs with the same form, which appear in different places in the word and have different functions or meanings. Does this provide a problem for the classical morpheme? Why (not)?

dɑ:nsə	'dancer'
draɪvə	'driver'
kɪlə	'killer'
prəvaɪdə	provider
wɜ:kə	'worker'
wɔ:kə	'walker'

əblu:m	'abloom'
əʤɑ:	'ajar'
əfləʊt	'afloat'
əgeɪp	'agape'
əmɪs	'amiss'
əsli:p	'asleep'

5. Metathesis is the process that inverts the order of two segments (usually adjacent segments) in a word. The English word *wasp* is cognate with the Danish word *hveps*, and shows that one of the languages has changed the original order of the /s/ and the /p/. The relationship between standard English *ask* and non-standard (but older) *ax* is also a matter of metathesis. In these examples, metathesis is purely phonological, but it is claimed, controversially, that metathesis may also be used for morphological purposes. An example from Saanich, a language of Vancouver Island, is provided below. The labels 'Actual' and 'Non-actual' refer to two distinct aspects of the verb. Only the stem° of the verbs is presented, and the stem may have other morphology attached to it in real usage. The abbreviation 's.th.' means 'something'.

Saanich

Non-actual	*Gloss*	*Actual*	*Gloss*
t'sə	'X breaks s.th.'	t'əs	'X is breaking s.th.'
q'kʷ'ə	'X straightens s.th.'	q'əkʷ'	'X is straightening s.th.'
tkʷə	'X breaks s.th.'	təkʷ	'X is breaking s.th.'
ʃʧ'ə	'X whips s.th.'	ʃəʧ'	'X is whipping s.th.'
tqʷə	'X tightens s.th.'	təqʷ	'X is tightening s.th.'

For some authorities (e.g. Anderson 1992), morphological metathesis such as would be involved in deriving the Actual form from the Non-actual form presents an argument against the classical notion of the morpheme, as it has been discussed in the chapter.

Why might it be an argument against the morpheme? Evaluate the force of this argument. Is there a possible analysis of this data which is compatible with the morpheme? Are there drawbacks to such an analysis, such that you would want to reject it? Could a morphemic analysis be saved in a slightly different version of what the morpheme entails?

The problem, though, is more complicated than this seems to imply. Stonham (1994: ch. 6) argues that there is no metathesis here, but both the Actual and the Non-actual forms are derived from an underlying form by purely phonological rules. Anderson (2005) rejects this analysis. In the light of this discussion, revisit your earlier conclusion on the strength of the argument against the morpheme provided by metathesis.

3 Word-based morphology

3.1 Introduction

How does the morphological component of a grammar fit together with the other components of a grammar? If we imagine a fairly standard generative syntax° such as has appeared in many guises since the early 1960s, the syntax will provide, as its output, a labelled tree. In all probability, the nodes of the tree will not only be associated with labels for word-classes°, but also a number of features° for categories such as number, tense, mood, aspect, person, case. These are termed 'morphosyntactic features°' because they are vital for the operation of the syntax (the syntax has to know what agrees° with what in terms of number, for example), but are also vital for the morphology, since the morphology has to specify the appropriate form of the word which will appear in the output of the tree. In other words, the syntax provides the semantic information required to specify which morphosyntactic word° is required, and it is the job of the morphology to use that information to provide an appropriate word-form°. What we assume we need is a way to get from some kind of identifier of the lexeme concerned (a basic form, a unique identifying number, or other identifying system) and the semantics of the grammatical word to a word-form.

Such a view of morphology came into existence alongside the types of generative grammar that it presupposes, although the underlying principles of such a grammar go further back to the approaches to the grammars of Greek and Latin taken in the classical period. Modern versions exist under various names, including Word-and-Paradigm grammar and A-morphous Morphology. Here the label 'Word-and-Paradigm' or 'WP' will be used to cover all such models.

3.2 The fundamentals of such a model

The most important point about a model of this kind is that its fundamental unit is the morphosyntactic word°. Specifically, it does not deal with morphemes. To go back to the simple example that was used at the beginning of Chapter 2, in a Word-and-Paradigm morphology, you cannot say that *cats* means 'more than one cat' because it contains an *-s* which means 'plural', you have to say that *cats* is the plural form of CAT. The distinction may seem small, but it has major implications for our view of the structures involved.

As set out above, the morphological component of such a grammar inherits a number of morphosyntactic features from the syntax. It also gains information on the form of stems and factors such as gender° or conjugation class° from the list of lexemes° in the dictionary or lexicon°. Accordingly, the way in which the rules determine the form of words depends upon a theory of features°, of which there are several. For the exposition here, we will use a system where the feature shows what Matthews (1974) calls the morphological category° and the particular morphological property° from that category that is to be marked. For instance, the word *swam* marks not only the lexeme SWIM, but also the morphological category of Tense°, in this instance specifically the property of the past tense. We can write this as [Tense: past].

In the light of the lexeme involved and the morphosyntactic features from the lexicon and the syntax, a series of rules builds up the phonological structure of any markers° required. The format of these rules is not of particular importance for the discussion of this approach, and there may be several ways of writing the required rule systems. But what is crucial is that the rules do not generate a series of morphemes, they generate a purely phonological structure. Consider some forms of the French verb DONNER 'to give' in (1).

(1)	donner	'to give'
	donnons	'we give'
	donnerai	'I shall give'
	donnions	'we were giving'
	donnerions	'we would give'

From the point of view of morpheme theory, it is clear that there are a number of recurrent elements in the word-forms presented in (1). In a Word-and-Paradigm morphology, the only division that is theoretically important is that between the stem *donn-* (which is an exponent° of the lexeme° DONNER) and the rest, which is an exponent of the various features whose meanings determine the construction of the morphosyntactic word. In cases like *swam*, even the distinction between stem and morphosyntactic features may be blurred or lost.

This has the great advantage that it avoids all the criticisms of the morpheme that were set out in Chapter 2. If there are no morphemes, the criticisms of the morpheme are irrelevant. What the model loses (if, indeed, it is a loss, given the problems that were set out in Chapter 2) is the ability to point at a portion of a word-form that is not a stem and say 'that bit means X'. It also means that the notion of allomorphy° is lost, since allomorphy depends upon there being a morpheme. The facts that are central to the notion of allomorphy are hidden in the rules constructing phonological form.

3.3 Two potential criticisms of word-based morphology

One of the criticisms often levelled at morphemic morphology from within Word-and-Paradigm is that morphemic morphology treats all languages as though they were agglutinative° languages. These are languages, and Turkish is often cited as a textbook example, in which every element of the word-form is well defined and corresponds to a single meaning. In English, a word like *unfriendliness*, which can be broken down into *un-*, *friend*, *-li* and *-ness*, provides a piece of agglutinative morphology. To phrase it differently: there is biuniqueness° between form° and meaning. Morphemic morphology, the criticism goes, makes all languages look as though they are of this type. But Word-and-Paradigm does the opposite: it makes all languages look as though they are fusional°, like Latin or Russian. These languages often have material in their morphological systems which does not allow for an analysis into uncontroversial concatenated elements each of which has its own meaning, and so they are precisely the languages which have been used in Chapter 2 to illustrate the shortcomings of the morpheme. The implication of this criticism is that it is better to treat Turkish as though it were Latin than it is to treat Latin like Turkish because there are languages in which the notion of the morpheme is problematic. This makes the assumption that we have to treat all languages the same way, and within the same theoretical framework. While that would no doubt be an ideal situation, if we have to choose between a theory which is consistent across languages and a good description of individual languages, it is not clear which is the better choice to make.

Another problem arises from the Word-and-Paradigm treatment of derivation. Word-and-Paradigm is fundamentally set up to deal with inflectional° morphology: the meaning side of the morphology is provided by morphosyntactic features°, such as [Tense°: present] or

[Case°: accusative°]. These are marked in the syntactic tree, and the phonological rules in the morphology interpret them in phonological terms. When it comes to derivational° morphology, though, there are no morphosyntactic features to interpret. The suffix in *Victoriana*, whose meaning ('collection of objects associated with ~') is perfectly transparent, cannot have that meaning represented as a morphosyntactic feature, (1) because there is no syntactic consequence of that meaning and (2), although this is less persuasive, because the meaning is rare, not generalisable, and not in any paradigm° of meanings. Even something which might look more grammatical, such as 'agent' in a word like *killer*, cannot be marked by a morphosyntactic feature because the word *killer* might not be an agent in the syntax (as in the sentence *The police shot the killer*, for example, where *killer* is a patient). This is not in dispute: Anderson (1992) says that the meaning side of derivational morphology is provided by whatever semantic theory the analyst might choose. The implication of this, though, is that there is a firm boundary between that morphology which interprets morphosyntactic features, and that which interprets other things such as derivational categories. The same conclusion is demanded by the fact that the interpretation of morphosyntactic features applies to lexemes°, with the stems° of the lexemes required as input to the rules which create the phonological form of the word-form°. For this to be true, derivation must be dealt with alongside the root and before inflection, even in those rare instances where the inflectional markers occur between the root and the derivational markers, as illustrated in (2).

(2) Dutch: *muzikant-en-dom* 'musician-PL-hood = musicianhood'
English: *better-ment, folk-s-y*
Breton: *tamm-où-ig-où* 'piece-PL-DIMINUTIVE-PL = little pieces' (Press 1986: 72)
Welsh: *merch-et-os* 'girl-PL-DIMINUTIVE = little girls'

All of this demands that there should be a clear-cut distinction between inflectional° and derivational° morphology (or, equivalently, between lexeme° and word-form°). This is the question which we will now consider.

3.4 Inflection and derivation

3.4.1 Questions of definition

Although it has not yet been spelt out explicitly, the distinction between word-form° and lexeme° is inherent in the distinction between inflection° and derivation°. Inflection produces word-forms of known lexemes; derivation produces new lexemes. Given that we have been operating with lexemes and word-forms, the distinction between inflection and derivation has been implicit in what has been said. But so far we have not had a definition of either the difference between word-form and lexeme, or the difference between inflection and derivation. If there is the possibility of confusion – as we shall see there is – we really need to be able to tell whether we are dealing with inflection or derivation.

It is, of course, perfectly valid to give an ostensive definition: to say that particular categories are inflectional while others are derivational by providing a list of which is which. Such a definition is not generalisable, though. If we find a language with a new category, how will we know whether that category is inflectional or derivational? Alternatively, we can see inflection and derivation as two distinct types, with some criterion or criteria which allow the linguist to sort categories into the two types. This is an Aristotelian definition, in terms of necessary and sufficient conditions. There is also a third type of definition, which sees categories not always as things which can be defined in this way, but as things defined by a number of conditions which apply to a greater or lesser extent. The categories themselves are called 'canonical° categories', and individual instantiations of the categories approximate more or less to the canonical version, where all the conditions are met. The question is whether inflection and derivation can be defined by necessary and sufficient conditions, or whether they are canonical categories.

In my view, the best set of necessary and sufficient conditions for distinguishing between inflection and derivation are the following:

(3) (a) Inflection is what is necessary for the syntax.
    (b) Inflection is obligatory.

Both of these require some explanation. The two go together, but we must try to split them up to some degree. If something is obligatory, it does not mean that it must have a marker° (e.g. an affix°). We have seen that some grammatical categories may be unmarked° (for instance, the nominative singular in masculine Russian nouns or the imperative in English verbs). What it means is that the grammar requires a choice of an appropriate form at that point in the construction°. So, in the Russian instance, the grammar needs to know that there is a masculine singular noun, even if there is no overt marker of that status, just as it needs to know that there is a genitive plural masculine noun (which does have an affix to show its status). With the English imperative, the grammar needs to know that the verb is imperative so that it knows that an overt subject for the verb is not required. The implication is that in the slot that requires a nominative singular noun, we must always have a noun which carries that information, whether it is marked overtly or not (for neuter and feminine nouns in Russian, it is overtly marked, for masculine nouns it is not). A noun which is not masculine or not singular or not nominative cannot occur in a slot in a sentence which is specified as requiring a masculine singular noun.

If something is necessary for the syntax, then the syntax cannot avoid showing the relevant category. There are some languages, like English, French, Latin, Russian and also a host of non-Indo-European languages round the world, where the syntax demands that tense should be specified, and other languages where this is not the case. In the first group, tense is inflectional; in the others, it is not. If a language in the first group has a present and a past tense, then whenever there is a tensed verb in the syntax, a choice between those two tenses will have to be made. This will be true, even where the two mean the same thing: *Shakespeare says you should neither borrow nor lend* and *Shakespeare said you should neither borrow nor lend*, for all practical purposes mean precisely the same thing, but you cannot have a version without tense marking, because tense marking is necessary for the syntax.

It turns out that there is a problem with this definition. The problem is this: if we change our notion of syntax, we change the notion of inflection. Consider the following example. In most versions of syntax for Indo-European languages, there is a distinction between nouns and verbs which is lexically determined. If something is a noun, it takes one set of inflections, if it is a verb, it takes another set. The distinction between nouns and verbs is thus something lexical°, something marked in the lexicon°, even though the syntax° will need to put the appropriate lexemes into the proper positions in the tree. However, Chomsky (1970) proposes a version of grammar where lexical entries are neutral between noun and verb. A pair of superficial distinctions such as *criticise* and *criticism* is something that is not in the fundamental semantic part of the lexicon, because both *criticise* and *criticism* take the same arguments: *Kim criticised my argument* and *Kim's criticism of my argument* show the same relationship between Kim, my argument and what Kim did to the argument. In that case, the superficial difference between *criticise* and *criticism*, the morphology, is something that the syntax needs to know about in order to place the item from the lexical entry (the thing which is neither a noun nor a verb, but neutral between them) in the appropriate part of the sentence. In other words, in this version of English grammar, the morphology reflected by the affixes° *-ise* and *-ism* is relevant to the syntax, and is thus inflectional. If this is the case, inflection and derivation are not categories inherent language; they are categories that the linguist imposes on the particular version of grammar that happens to be in use.

The alternative, canonical view sees inflection and derivation as categories of languages which may not be identical in all languages, but which must be describable in terms of their functions. In this view, there are a number of criteria which canonical inflection will meet and which canonical derivation will meet, but not only may there be exceptions within a given language, different languages may draw a distinction that is important for that language at different points along the scale between them. The set of criteria that are used to show the distinction is large, and not all authorities agree on the relative importance of the various criteria. However, they include criteria like those in (4).

(4) (a) Inflection is obligatory, derivation is not.
(b) Inflection is semantically regular, derivation may not be.
(c) Inflection is formally regular, derivation may not be.
(d) Inflection is fully productive°, that is, it can typically be used freely on any available base; derivation is typically not, so that there are unpredictable gaps in sets of derivatives.
(e) Where both inflection and derivation are present in the same word-form, the marker° of derivation is closer to the root than the marker of inflection (though note the exceptions in (2) above).
(f) Derivation may cause a change in word-class°, inflection does not.
(g) The meaning associated with derivational morphology is more lexical° and less grammatical, and also less generalisable° across bases, than is the meaning associated with inflectional morphology; the meaning of inflectional morphology allows the fundamental meaning of the lexeme to be contextualised.

These criteria, it is important to stress, are not exhaustive, but are representative of those given in the literature. We can see how they work if we apply them to two test cases from English, the case of -*ly*$]_{\text{ADV}}$ and the case of -*ing*. In both these instances, we will see, it is not absolutely clear whether they are cases of inflection or of derivation.

Example 1: Adverbial -ly

Adverbial -*ly* creates adverbs from corresponding adjectives, such as *abruptly, prettily, stupidly, supposedly, wisely*. There is a homophonous° -*ly* which creates adjectives from nouns (*deathly*, *friendly*, *manly*, *masterly*, *nightly*) which we assume is completely separate and irrelevant for our discussion.

In an attempt to see whether this *-ly* is inflectional or derivational, we can try to apply the criteria outlined in (4).

Adverbial *-ly* is semantically and formally regular. Its form is always *-ly* (with some minor differences in pronunciation from dialect to dialect). It always has the same meaning, which we can gloss as 'in a ~ manner', except in a very few words, the most notable of which is *hardly*. *Hardly* is an adverb, as we would expect, but does not mean 'in a hard manner', as the T-shirt slogan *I've been working hardly* makes clear. Another such example is *barely*. In terms of criteria (b) and (c) in (4), this is compatible with *-ly* being inflectional, but also compatible with it being derivational.

In general terms, *-ly* is productive°. If you meet a new adjective which is unfamiliar to you, say *hircine*, you will automatically expect there to be a corresponding adverb *hircinely*. However, there are some gaps in the paradigm°: *early*, *fast*, *fair*, *loud*, for instance, can be adjectives or adverbs without any *-ly*. Where there is an option to use the *-ly* form, it may be synonymous°, as in *She wouldn't play fair/fairly*, *He shouted loud/loudly to be heard over the din*, but may not, as in *They screamed out loud/loudly*, *He's fair/fairly clever* (where *fair* may be dialectal but is a booster°, while *fairly* is a downtoner°). The addition of *-ly* to bases that end in *-(l)y* is no longer as acceptable as it once was, and words like *dailily*, *oilily*, *sillily*, *uglily* are usually avoided, and on some occasions (and in some varieties) the adjective may also be used as an adverb: *New stock arriving weekly!* In colloquial English, some adjectives are used in place of adverbs when modifying adjectives: *bloody/fucking/pretty/real stupid*. In terms of criterion (d) of (4), this is largely compatible with *-ly* being inflectional, but could be taken to suggest that *-ly* is derivational. The example of modifiers to adjectives could be taken as evidence of lack of obligatoriness in terms of criterion (a), but it is not a general lack of obligatoriness, just one in specific places.

The evidence from ordering (criterion (e)) is inconclusive. While *-ly* is always the last affix in a word, this is compatible both with it being inflectional and with it being derivational.

The crucial question is the question of word-class° (criterion (f)). Do adjectives and adverbs belong to the same word-class or to different word-classes? For the most part, adjectives and adverbs are in complementary distribution°, and could belong to the same word-class°. As was noted above, in many cases where both can occur, there is no significant difference between them, and they could just be stylistic variants.

This accounts for things like *Kiss me quick/quickly*, *Do it slow/slowly*. Nevertheless, there are places where this complementary distribution seems to be broken (Payne et al. 2010).

(5) The conclusion was plain daft/plainly daft
I want her desperate/desperately
Dinner will be short/shortly
He made the robot clever/cleverly
She left the house quiet/quietly

This point remains one of controversy in the literature. But even if we take the view that adjective and adverb are, as is implied by the labels, distinct word-classes, a suggestion has been made by some scholars that where other factors suggest that something is inflectional, it should be possible to allow for word-class-changing inflection. If we allow for that point of view, the value of criterion (f) is put in doubt.

The evidence from the meaning of *-ly* (criterion (g)) is also not clear enough to lead to a firm decision. Obviously, the meaning 'adverb' can be argued to be grammatical, but so can the meaning 'adjective' in *parental* or 'noun' in *amusement*, and these are typically treated as derivational. If the meaning 'adverb' is inflectional in *prettily*, what about the prefix *a-* which also creates adverbs, for example in *aboard* and *aground*? Yet inflection in English is never otherwise prefixal.

Overall we have a situation here where there is only weak justification for deciding that *-ly*$]_{ADV}$ is inflectional or that it is derivational, and we find authorities taking both sides of the debate. What this means is that the border between the two is not always clear-cut. Grammars can treat *-ly* affixation as either, but the decision is not because the language necessarily draws a clear line between the two categories. In more general terms, the criteria for inflection and derivation do not always provide clear answers as to which category applies.

Example 2: The suffix -ing

There are various uses of a suffix *-ing*, as indicated in (6). It can be part of a verb, it can be found on something that is to some extent (perhaps entirely) nominal, and it can be found on things which are used as adjectives. The question the linguist first has to answer is: how many homophonous° *-ing* affixes are there?

(6) Her Majesty is cutting the ribbon (verbal construction)
Cutting the cake (quickly), she served it up (non-finite verbal construction)
That was a (very) cutting remark (adjective)

Kim's (quick) cutting of the cake defused the situation (verbal and nominal aspects)
The (quick) cutting of the cake defused the situation (slightly more nominal construction)
The train disappeared into the (deep) cutting (noun)

The answer is not necessarily obvious. There is a single suffix form, with some socially based variation between pronunciations /ɪŋ/ and /ɪn/, but no regular allomorphy° at all (criterion (c)). The form is highly productive°, being found on any non-modal verb, though not necessarily in all possible usages (criterion (d)). Whatever the meaning of the affix is taken to be, it is grammatical rather than lexical (criterion (g)), but hard to pin down. In terms of criterion (e), the only affixes which can occur further from the root than *-ing* are *-s* (in forms like *meetings*), *-ly* (in forms like *surprisingly*) and, for some speakers, *-est* (in forms like *winningest*), all of which are, or may be considered to be, inflectional and so do not give good evidence for the status of *-ing*. All of this suggests not only that we have a single affix, but that it is inflectional.

On the other hand, *-ing* can create a verb-form from a verbal base (which sounds inflectional) or create a noun from a verbal base (which sounds derivational), and because it can do both, it sounds as if there must be at least two separate affixes here. One of the benefits of the word-based morphology approach is that we do not really have to decide about how many morphemes or affixes there are, but we do still have to decide whether this is inflectional morphology or derivational morphology.

There may be an argument that all these *-ing* forms are derivational, although it may not be strong. First of all, we are, etymologically° speaking, dealing with two distinct affixes here. In current German, a related language, we find the work of English *-ing* distributed between a suffix *-ung* (as in *Schreibung* 'writing') and a suffix *-end* (as in *wütend* 'fierce, raging'). The first of these is usually considered derivational, the latter inflectional. Etymologically, therefore, it might not be surprising to find that that there is a split in functions. However, we are dealing with morphology and not with etymology°. Not only is it not clear that there are sufficient traces of this division left for modern speakers of English to distinguish between the two, but at some point in the history of English, speakers must have felt they were doing the same job for the forms to have merged. Second, there used to be, and in some varieties still is, a verbal form with a prefixed *a-*: *a-hunting we will go, the times they are a-changin'*. This *a-* is a reduced form of the preposition *on*, and so there must at one stage have been (and possibly still is for those who use this form regularly) an understanding that the word ending in *-ing* is a noun and not a verb. If that is the case, we could argue that *-ing* is always derivational, because it always changes the word-class of the base to which it is attached. But this does not accord with the generally accepted position that in the verbal construction with *-ing* illustrated in the first example in (6), the *-ing* form is a verb. We would have to say that the form of BE is the verb, and that BE forms a construction° with the *-ing* nominalisation°, and that such a construction has an unpredictable aspectual meaning. The argument is weak because it does not take account of the intuitions of modern speakers of English; it does have the advantage, though, of providing a coherent account of the use of *-ing* in terms of inflection and derivation.

Even if we accept the view that all the uses of *-ing* are derivational (despite a general consensus to the contrary), we have still not answered the question of how many suffixes there are with the same form. Is the fact that *-ing* forms adjectives in some places and noun-y things in others sufficient to say that it is (at least) two distinct affixes? Or should we argue, on the basis of *intellectual*, which can be an adjective (*an intellectual argument*) or a noun (*only an intellectual would make that distinction*), that the same affix can mark either adjective or noun? There is another option here: perhaps one of the forms in *-ing* is basic, and the others are derived from it by conversion°.

Overall, the debate becomes incredibly difficult to evaluate, and individual solutions are made less secure by the number of potential options on offer. The standard criteria (like those in (4)) provide some help, but not enough for us to feel certain that we can use them consistently or coherently. How do we deal with the situation when the criteria which apply do not agree? For example, if we have to give one criterion priority in the discussion of adverbial *-ly*, does the same criterion get priority in the discussion of *-ing*, and does that make sense of the data?

Where the Word-and-Paradigm model is concerned, the main focus on *-ing* will arise only if we consider it to be inflectional. But we still have a situation where what is inflectional and what is derivational are not easily distinguished, and this is, in itself, problematic for the Word-and-Paradigm model, which makes the assumption that we can always tell inflection and derivation apart.

3.4.2 The inflection–derivation split

While the examples that have been discussed above are notorious for their difficulty in terms of inflection and derivation, and while it is true that there are huge numbers of examples – especially in some language types – which are not at all controversial, it is the awkward instances which provide the test of a theory. At the very least, these examples seem to show that there is no easily determinable algorithm which will allow a decision on whether a particular piece of morphology is inflectional or derivational, and the implication of this is that any model of morphology which presupposes a straightforward division between inflection and derivation is built on unstable ground.

In recent years that picture has been changed slightly by the division of inflection into contextual inflection° and inherent inflection° (Booij 1996). Contextual inflection is that part of the morphology which is determined by agreement° (whether by concord° or by government°). So plural marking on Latin adjectives when they modify plural nouns is a matter of contextual inflection, as is the use of the accusative case° on the direct object of most transitive verbs in Latin. Inherent inflection is that part of morphology which is obligatory in the sentence, but where the speaker can choose one of two or more meaningful options. The difference between the French sentences in (7) is a matter of tense: tense is obligatory in the sentence, but which tense is selected is a meaningful choice.

(7) Le monsieur donne le cadeau à sa fille
'The gentleman gives/is giving the present to his daughter'
Le monsieur donna le cadeau à sa fille
'The gentleman gave the present to his daughter'
Le monsieur donnera le cadeau à sa fille
'The gentleman will give the present to his daughter'

Although such a division is helpful in a number of regards, any new subcategorisation leads to more borderline cases. In this particular instance, tense is inherent inflection, but it is presumably contextual in places where it is determined by sequence of tenses. So if Chris and Lee say to a friend 'We can come tomorrow', that friend might report it as *They said they could come tomorrow*. But that report is vague, because it would equally be true if they had actually said 'We could come tomorrow'. The choice for Chris and Lee is meaningful, but the reporting friend is constrained by sequence of tenses, and has no choice. This innovation may, therefore, simply make it even more difficult to determine what category a particular instance belongs to.

3.5 What if there is no inflection–derivation split?

The implications of calling into question the division between inflection and derivation are huge. Not only does it seem to imply that a model which deals exclusively with inflection is impossible, it seems to imply that all morphology is fundamentally of the same type, and that morphological structures with affixes can all be seen as being variable along certain parameters, but not so different as to require different handling within a grammar. Implicitly, this is the view within morpheme-based morphology: the distinction between inflection and derivation is a secondary distinction imposed on an analysis into morphs° and morphemes°, not the basis on which morphology is built. If this assumption is part of the baggage of some views of morphology, it is not a particularly surprising view, in one sense. Nevertheless, it is worth considering whether it is a tenable view. We shall have to return to this question in a later chapter as well (Section 7.5.3), but we can make a first attempt at this point.

The first point that is often raised in this context is that there are no special morphological processes which apply only in inflection or only in derivation. Prefixation, suffixation, other types of affixation, no marking at all, reduplication, internal modification can all be used apparently inflectionally or derivationally in various languages. So even though it seems to be the case that in English there is no inflectional prefixation, this is not a restriction on languages, but merely a curious fact about English. Even cumulative exponence° can be found in derivation if we take it that *song* is a single morph related to *sing*. Furthermore, phenomena such as suppletion and syncretism can also be found in both inflection and derivation. Suppletion° exists when the root in a word in some forms of the paradigm is not clearly related to the root in the rest of the paradigm. A classic case is *went*, which acts as the past tense of GO, but which is not phonologically related to *go* (historically, *went* comes from a different verb from *go*). As a corresponding derivational instance, someone who comes from Texas is called a *Texan* (with clearly related roots°), but someone who comes from Indiana is called a *Hoosier* (with an unrelated root). Syncretism° occurs when different forms in a paradigm have precisely the same form despite meaning different things. In Latin neuter nominal declensions, for instance, the nominative and accusative singular forms of nouns are the same: *bellum* 'war' can mean 'the nominative singular of BELLUM' or 'the accusative singular of BELLUM'. The same syncretism is found only very rarely in nouns of other declensions. In English derivation, the word *boiler* can mean 'a machine which boils' or 'something which is intended to be boiled' (as when *boiler* means 'boiling fowl'): here the same form can be the thing that does the boiling or the thing that gets boiled. We can contrast this with *employer* and *employee* where the same semantic relationship is marked by different affixes. It also happens, both in inflection and in derivation, that sometimes an expected form in the paradigm is missing. For example, *beware* exists mainly as an imperative, though it is also found as an infinitive. But it has no third person singular form or past tense: **He always bewares the ides of March*; **She told me to beware, so I bewared.* In derivation this behaviour is more expected. We have a word *hateful*, but *loveful* is not a standard word.

Because inflectional morphology is usually fully productive°, we expect that if case° is marked on some masculine nouns in Latin or Russian, it will be marked on all of them, and that each noun will have a form for each of the cases. There will be no gaps, and we will be able to set out a paradigm° of forms, like that in (4) of Chapter 2, and find that paradigm filled for every noun. If, in contrast, there are places where derivational morphology is not fully productive (see (4) above in this chapter), it may be unrealistic to set out a paradigm of forms for derivational morphology. This is a standard position in current morphological thinking (though not a universal one): paradigms are a feature of inflectional morphology only.

But if we do not distinguish between inflection and derivation, then the implication is that either there are no paradigms in either inflection or derivation, or there are paradigms in both. We have to ask, if we say that we expect every verb to have a third person singular present tense form, a past tense form and a past participle, can we not also say that we expect every verb to have a nominalisation°, an agent form, if transitive a corresponding *-able* form, and so on? The paradigms in derivation provide less sureness of prediction than inflectional paradigms, but the general idea seems reasonable. And just as we cannot tell from general rules that the past tense of LEAVE will be *left* but the past tense of BELIEVE will be *believed*, so we cannot tell by general principles that the nominalisation of *refer* will be *referral* but the nominalisation of *confer* will be *conferment.* There are arguments against this position as well, but there is some justification for saying that the notion of paradigm is not unique to inflection.

But if there are factors like these similarities in behaviour which might make us think that discarding the inflection–derivation distinction would be useful, there are others which might make us revise that idea.

Most obviously, the notions of lexemes° and morphosyntactic words° are intimately tied to the notion of inflection. If there is no difference between inflection and derivation, we cannot distinguish lexemes and morphosyntactic words, and we have to make do with word-forms°. This is important since, even among people who are not language professionals, there is a feeling that *infer*, *infers* and *inferred* are 'the same word' in a way that *employable*, *employer* and *employee* are not. Without the notion of lexeme, we have no way to capture that insight.

The second point is more difficult to explain, but is to do with automaticity. Consider the word *Trumaniana*, which I doubt you will find in any dictionary. Its meaning is probably reasonably clear: 'a collection of artefacts connected with someone famous called Truman (perhaps the Yorkshire cricketer Fred Truman, perhaps the American president, Harry Truman, perhaps someone else)'. Despite the meaning of this new word being relatively easy to work out, we do not feel that there is automatically an *-(i)ana* word corresponding to every single name that we know. Even if there exists a huge collection of artefacts connected with Elvis Presley, we do not necessarily think of these as being *Elvisiana* or *Presleyana*. The same is not true of inflections. Once we have a word *utopify* (attested, but probably not familiar), we know absolutely that there is a word *utopifies* and another *utopified*. In English, where the number of words we can predict in this way is extremely small, this may not seem particularly interesting. But in languages like Russian or Finnish, the number of forms that automatically exist the moment you find a new verb runs into the hundreds or thousands, and in Archi, a language of the Caucasus, it said to reach 1.5 million (Kibrik 1998: 467). This has huge implications for the way in which we imagine words are stored in the memories of real speakers. If it were the case that on hearing a new verb a speaker had to calculate and list in memory all 1.5 million forms of that verb, we would expect an appreciable pause in the conversation every time a speaker meets a new verb. That does not happen, and we can be fairly sure that some of the forms of the verb among the 1.5 million are so rare that they might not occur in a speaker's lifetime. Our only option is to assume that a speaker has the ability to create the appropriate word-form when it is required. That is precisely the ability that a Word-and-Paradigm grammar tries to emulate. The Word-and-Paradigm grammar does not attempt to model the creation of a word like *Trumaniana* because it sees such creations as different in nature, because less automatically available, than words like *utopifies*. It certainly seems that the creation of words like *Trumaniana*, the products of derivation, are more open to introspection, less frequent and perhaps harder to produce than inflected words. Consider, for instance, the quotations from fiction in (8), which seem to reflect a rather common experience.

(8) (a) She . . . pulled on another pair of disposable gloves. Gemma wondered if there was a proper name for a glovophiliac. (Gabrielle Lord, *Baby Did a Bad Bad Thing*, Sydney: Hodder, 2002, p. 272)

(b) "They're moist and cinnamony and . . . is that a word?"
"Is what a word?"
"Cinnamony."
Hannah laughed. "If it's not, it ought to be." (Joanne Fluke, *Lemon Meringue Pie Murder*, New York: Kensington, 2003, p. 217)

(c) "He knew he wasn't going to get a penny out of Bairn, so he sent his chief crucifixionist to make an example."
Loudermilk wiped the legs of his glasses. "I don't think that's a word." (Loren D. Estleman, *American Detective*, New York: Doherty, 2007, p. 125)

(d) "I'd need an enforcement arm. For my benignity, I mean. If that's a word."
"It should be," Tamara said. (John Lescroart, *The Hunter*, New York: Dutton, 2012, p. 139)

(e) She had always been one of the popular kids – not the leader, not the trendsetter just . . . a belonger, she thought, knowing that wasn't a real word. It should have been. (Tami Hoag, *The 9th Girl*, New York: Dutton, 2013, p. 151)

There is also evidence from a range of languages that speakers learn to use derivational morphology productively later than they learn to use inflectional morphology, fail to recognise derivational morphology in words, lose derivational morphology in language death situations, and that in some cultures the invention of new words is socially constrained (see Bauer 1996 for some discussion). The evidence is not unambiguously in favour of a distinction between inflection and derivation, but much of the evidence is compatible with such a distinction.

So now we are in a situation where we have two conflicting views, both with some supporting evidence. On the one hand, it seems that the distinction between inflection and derivation is messy, and it may not be possible to make consistent decisions about which category certain morphological processes belong to in individual languages. Indeed, it may be possible to manipulate the definitions of inflection and derivation in individual languages, depending on the form of the grammar being presented. This casts doubt over the validity of the distinction, although proof of a messy division does not in itself prove that the distinction is untenable. On the other hand, there is some evidence of a rather different type, based fundamentally on the behaviour of speakers, which suggests that the division between inflection and derivation may be useful and, at some level, valid.

Such a situation does not provide a reason for panic, but it does mean that we need to look for further evidence and look for new interpretations of the data which may help resolve the issue.

Notes and comments

On the use of constructions° in morphological description, see Booij (2010). The idea in construction grammar is that individual items frequently enter into specific collocations in which their meaning becomes changed and unpredictable. The constructions thus created are not subject to the same kinds of semantic rules which allow the interpretation of elements in a sentence from the lexically listed meaning of each of its elements and the meaning of the syntactic relationship holding between them.

On the morphology of Archi, see Kibrik (1998).

Reading

For an elaborated Word-and-Paradigm grammar, see Matthews (1972) – though Matthews sets out the principles in a number of other publications, including Matthews (1974). For A-morphous Morphology, see Anderson (1992). The label 'Word-and-Paradigm' seems to stem from Hockett ([1954] 1957).

For criteria on inflection and derivation, see in particular Plank (1994), who provides the most complete list of criteria for making the distinction. Most textbooks provide a subset of these criteria, though not necessarily phrased in the same way.

For the argument on adjectives and adverbs, see Payne et al. (2010) and Giegerich (2012). On the view for allowing word-class-changing inflection, see Haspelmath (1996).

On derivational paradigms, see Štekauer (2014).

Discussion questions

Some suggested answers to these questions can be found in the Answers to Discussion Questions at edinburghuniversitypress.com/rethinkingmorphology

1. Consider the data from written French below. How would you account for such data in a morpheme-based morphology as opposed to in a Word-and-Paradigm morphology? While you may choose to formulate specific rules, if you wish, the core of the exercise lies in

seeing how the two models differ in what they say about the data. What advantages do you see to either of the treatments? Would a morphomic treatment be helpful?

je donne	'I give'
je donnais	'I used to give'
je donnai	'I gave'
je donnerai	'I shall give'
je donnerais	'I would give'
je parle	'I speak'
je parlais	'I used to speak'
je parlai	'I spoke'
je parlerai	'I shall speak'
je parlerais	'I would speak'

2. Consider the data below from Turkish and from Latin. Compare the way in which such data would be handled in a morpheme-based morphology and in a Word-and-Paradigm morphology. What advantages are there for each approach? This question is open-ended. If you consult grammars of Turkish and Latin, you will find that there are more patterns than are illustrated here. In Latin there are other declensions; in Turkish there are more phonologically conditioned allomorphs. The apparent benefits of the two approaches may change when more data is added.

Turkish

el	'hand (nominative)'
eli	'hand (accusative)'
ele	'hand (dative)'
elde	'hand (locative)'
eller	'hands (nominative)'
elleri	'hands (accusative)'
ellere	'hands (dative)'
ellerde	'hands (locative)'
evi	'house (accusative)'
evlerde	'houses (locative)'

Latin

puella	'girl (nominative)'
puellam	'girl (accusative)'
puellae	'girl (dative)'
puellā	'girl (ablative)'
puellae	'girls (nominative)'
puellās	'girls (accusative)'

puellīs	'girls (dative)'
puellīs	'girls (ablative)'
mēnsam	'table (accusative)'
mēnsīs	'tables (ablative)'

3. Consider the phrases in (a) and (b).

   (a) Kim's criticism of my argument.
   (b) Kim's view of my argument.

   Criticism has a morphological structure, but *view* does not. How will a Word-and-Paradigm grammar generate the word *criticism* in (a)? How will (b) be different? Assume that the meaning of the *-ism* is 'nominalisation'.

4. Is the past participle in English inflectional or derivational? Consider the data presented below and any other data from English you find relevant. (You will need to consider whether the data below is all relevant or not.) How sure are you of your answer? Is there an alternative position?

   (a) A bearded man was sitting in the corner.
   (b) A learned professor could not answer such stupid questions.
   (c) Don't mock the afflicted.
   (d) Goats have cloven hoofs.
   (e) He has a cleft palate.
   (f) He has killed the conversation.
   (g) He has learnt/learned the answers by heart.
   (h) He's just a very excited kid.
   (i) His dejectedness was visible to us all.
   (j) It was a foregone conclusion.
   (k) She has excited attention.
   (l) She is a skilled worker.
   (m) She sighed exaggeratedly.
   (n) The court has spoken.
   (o) The disabled have particular educational needs.
   (p) The dog barked excitedly.
   (q) The markedness of this construction explains its rarity.
   (r) The spoken word is not necessarily less important than the written word.
   (s) The undecideds will determine the outcome of the election.
   (t) There's a one-eyed yellow idol.
   (u) They had just spat/spit on the ground, and glared at us.
   (v) We have forgone our payments.
   (w) What shall we do with the drunken sailor?

5. Consider the data below from English, and feel free to add any extra data from English that you are familiar with. Is the category of plural (as added to nouns) in English inflectional or derivational? How do you determine an answer? Can you rule out the opposing answer?

singular form	*plural form*
?	clothes
?	dregs
?	mumps
?	scissors
alumnus	alumni
arm	arms
brother	brothers, brethren
crisis	crises
criterion, criteria	criteria, criterias, criterions
custom	customs
goose	geese, gooses
kanban	kanbans (see Knowles 1997 for the meaning)
kibbutz	kibbutzim, kibbutzes
knowledge	?
minute	minutes
mouse	mice, mouses, mices, meeces
music	?
octopus	octopuses, octopodes, octopi
person	people
salmon	salmon
sheep	sheep
soprano	sopranos, soprani

Consider also words like *folksy, gutsy, newsy, outdoorsy, sudsy.*

Consult any good grammar of English, such as Quirk et al. (1985), for further data. Beard (1982) discusses this question, but not with specific reference to English.

4 Word syntax

4.1 Introduction

There are many approaches to morphology, and one which provides a notable contrast with the word-based morphology discussed in the last chapter is known as the Syntax of Words. The label is given because it attempts to deal with morphology according to the fundamental principles that are accepted in syntax°. In particular, it views morphological structures as being made up of hierarchically organised strings of morphs° or morphemes° in the same way as sentences are. One of the main points of contrast with word-based morphology is that it treats inflection and derivation in the same way, as far as is possible, and so allows us to see what happens when we ignore inflection versus derivation as a major division in morphology. But as word syntax deals with sequences of elements, it involves morphs (and probably morphemes) just like morpheme-based morphology does.

As with the other theories discussed here, there is not just one model of word syntax available in the literature, there are several, and the presentation below will focus on those aspects of word syntax which these models share, rather than presenting just one of them.

4.2 Some basics

Consider the words *unfriendly* and *dishonesty*. Both are made up of a sequence of three morphs, but the structure is different in the two cases. *Unfriendly* is the negative of *friendly*, while *dishonesty* is the nominalisation° of *dishonest*. That is, the bracketings are different: *un[friend-ly]* and *[dis-honest]y*. To some extent we know this because of the possibility of *friendly*, but the non-existence of a noun *unfriend*. But in the *dishonesty* case both *dishonest* and *honesty* exist independently, and we are guided by the semantics of the construction: the whole word means 'the quality of being dishonest'. In some cases, qualities of an affix can help: *un-* attaches freely to adjectives, but less frequently to nouns, and then with rather different semantics (Bauer et al. 2013).

These examples show that a similar syntagmatic° structure can have a different hierarchical structure, which is related to a different semantic interpretation. This is just the same as we see in the distinction between, say, *red sky [at night]* and *female [person of interest]* in syntax°. The major difference is that in dealing with something like *unfriendly*, we are dealing with some obligatorily bound morphs°, while in the syntax we are dealing with words. And in the same way that a prefix *un-* leads us to expect an adjective in the base (although other possibilities are available), so the difference between *total political knowledge* and *totally political knowledge* is signalled because an adjective (*total*) makes us expect a noun, while an adverb (*totally*) makes us expect a verb or adjective, and so we get different bracketings again: *total [political knowledge]*, *[totally political] knowledge.*

In effect, then, the proposal in word syntax is that syntactic trees should not stop at the word level, but should continue within the word, with the same principles which govern syntactic structures also governing morphological structures. That is, instead of having a tree like that in (1) for the sentence *Realists dislike falsehoods*, we should have a tree rather more like that in (2). (Both trees miss out a great deal of information, but the general point should be clear.)

(1)

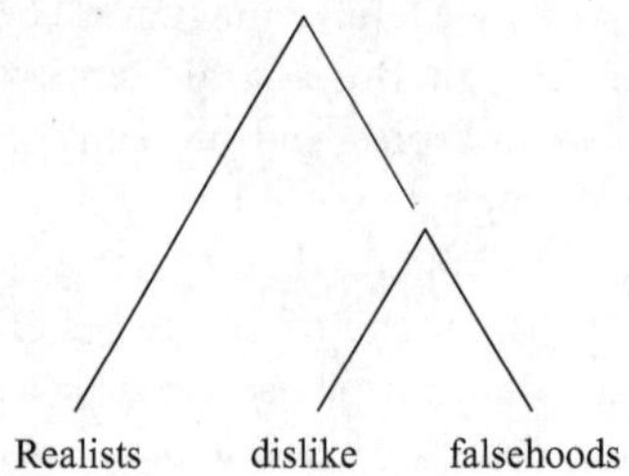

(2)

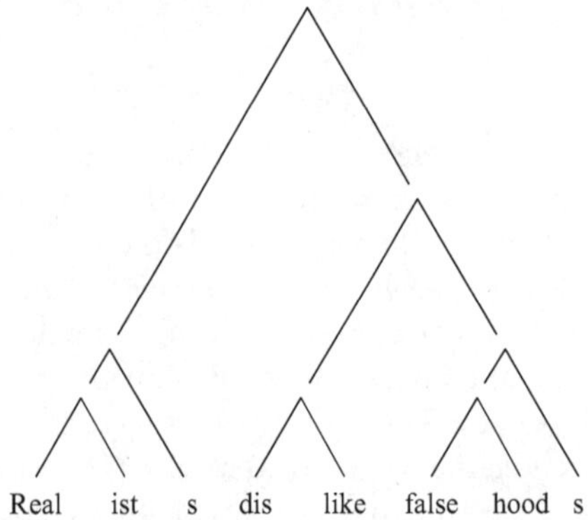

The obvious question is whether there is anything to be gained from this, and the answer is at least a provisional affirmative. There are many places in a number of languages where morphological structures have syntactic counterparts. In English, one of the most obvious examples is the difference between *more common* and *commoner*. *More common* and *commoner* are both perfectly good English, and mean precisely the same thing: *Diminutives are more common in Italian than in English* means just the same as *Diminutives are commoner in Italian than in English*. There are places in English where the two constructions are probably in complementary distribution° (so that one might be considered, in morphological terms, an allomorph° of the other), but there are also some places, as has just been illustrated, where either can occur without any semantic difference. We would probably not get *That man is intelligenter than my mum*, but if we did, we would be able to work out what it must mean. Because *more* and *common* are generally seen as being separate words in English, but *common* and *-er* belong to the same word, *more common* is generally thought of as being a piece of syntax, while *commoner* represents a morphological construction°. So here we have a case where morphology and syntax share a single construction type ('the comparative°') between them, in ways which are not entirely predictable. A rather similar example comes from the French tense° system. Most French tenses are shown by inflections on the verb. Corresponding to the verb DONNER 'to give' we have third person tensed forms like *donne* 'he/she/it gives', *donnait* 'he/she/it was giving', *donnera* 'he/she/it will give', *donnerait* 'he/she/it would give' and in formal written French, *donna* 'he/she/it gave'. But in modern colloquial French, we also have *a donné* 'he/she/it gave' where the *a* is third person singular present tense of the auxiliary verb AVOIR 'to have'. So while most of the tense system is dealt with by the morphological component (if it is separate from the syntactic component), the perfect, the *a donné* form, is dealt with by the syntax. Again, a single category, tense, is spread across morphology and syntax, and it might make better sense to treat them together.

Another place where syntax and morphology apparently overlap is when adjectives interact with compounds°. In order to understand this interaction we need to make two assumptions. The first is that the spelling of compounds is inconsistent in English, and *coffeepot*, *coffee-pot* and *coffee pot* are all found, even in dictionaries. Thus some compounds are written as though they are two orthographic words°, even if we might want to say (with any of these spellings) that there is a single lexeme° COFFEE-POT (which we might not know how to spell). The variable spelling is well attested and not controversial: there is a question as to whether different spellings imply different analyses, but the claim here is that there are no very good grounds for assuming that the three spellings of *coffee-pot* indicate different structures. The second assumption is that compounding is a morphological process. The assumption implicitly makes the claim (already made just above) that an item like COFFEE-POT is a lexeme, albeit one whose constituent elements are words of some kind. This claim is supported by the point that there is a certain amount of isolation involved in compounding. For example, if we compare the syntactic phrase *A black bird* with the compound *a blackbird*, one of the differences between the two is that in the compound we cannot make *black* comparative° or submodify it: **the blackerbird*, **the very blackbird.* We can do both of those things in syntax. Where the compound is made up of two nouns, as in *coffee-pot, carpark, windmill*, and so on, the first noun tends to be uninflectable (**coffee's pot*, **cars park*, **windsmill* – though note *arms race, suggestions box*), cannot take a determiner of its own and usually does not refer to a particular real-world entity. So we cannot have **the my carpark*, even if understood as 'the parking place for my car', and a *carpark* is a place for parking cars (in general) rather than a place for parking the Mazda with the licence plate TY2076.

On the basis of these two assumptions, we can look at the way in which compounds interact with adjectives. Consider the compound *history teacher.* If we add the adjective *French*, we have two possible readings: either we have a history teacher who is French, or we have a teacher of French history. In writing you cannot distinguish the two parsings of *French history teacher*, and you may or may not make a distinction between them in speech. So the adjective can modify the first element in the compound or the compound as a whole. But the addition of the adjective is syntax, while we have been assuming that compounding is morphology. If the two interact in this way, might it not be better to deal with the two in the same way, without splitting it across two different modules of the grammar?

At some level, therefore, we have reasons for considering the treatment of morphology as a part of syntax, and not as a separate component of the grammar. This has the benefit over word-based morphology (Chapter 3) that derivational as well as inflectional morphology is dealt with in the same way, but it does have many of the problems we have seen with morphemes, because it implies that we can break the word into a sequence of morphs. The word-syntax approach gives rise to a number of theoretical issues, of which just two will be considered here, neither of which has already been discussed: headedness and morphotactics. We will deal with each of these in turn.

4.3 Headedness

What makes a noun phrase a noun phrase? One of the obvious answers is that it contains a noun. But, we might argue, a verb phrase like *know the answer* also contains a noun. The point about a noun phrase is that it has a noun which is, in one terminology, the centre of the phrase. We can give that notion of centrality some content with a series of criteria which, in general terms, work together and where each implies the other. The element which meets all the criteria is called the 'head' of the phrase in which it occurs. The criteria which we shall consider are the following:

(a) The head of a phrase determines the word-class of the phrase in which it occurs.
(b) The head of a phrase is obligatory within the phrase in which it occurs.
(c) The head of the phrase is semantically a superordinate° term for the phrase as a whole (or, equivalently, the phrase as a whole is a hyponym° of the head of the phrase).
(d) The head of the phrase has the distribution of the phrase as a whole.
(e) Where relevant, the head of the phrase determines the morphological form of other elements within the phrase.

Consider the way in which these criteria work with reference to two simple phrases, *red bananas* and *extraordinarily stupid. Red bananas* is a noun phrase, and *bananas* is the only noun in the phrase; *extraordinarily stupid* is an adjective phrase and *stupid* may be the only adjective within it or both words may be adjectives (see the discussion of whether *-ly* adverbs are part of the same word-class as adjectives in Section 3.4.1). Under either result, it is *stupid* which makes *extraordinarily stupid* an adjective phrase. This means that in terms of criterion (a), *bananas* and *stupid* are the heads of their respective phrases. Anywhere we can have the phrase *red bananas* we can have the phrase *bananas*, and anywhere we can have the phrase *extraordinarily stupid* we can have the phrase *stupid*; we cannot replace these phrases with *red* or with *extraordinarily*, respectively. In terms of criterion (b), this again means that *bananas* and *stupid* are the heads of their phrases. The same observations can be used under criterion (d). If we can miss out *red* and *extraordinarily*, then the words that are left have the same distribution as the phrases we started with. *Red bananas* is a hyponym of *bananas*; *extraordinarily stupid* is a sub-type of *stupid*, and so *bananas* and *stupid* are yet again picked out as heads, this time by criterion (c). In English, *bananas* does not determine the morphological shape of *red*, but if we had a language (like Italian, German, Russian) where adjectives agree with nouns in gender° and/or case° and/or number, that would be true. If we believe that *-ly* is an inflection on adjectives, then *stupid* determines the form of *extraordinarily*. Otherwise, this criterion, criterion (e), fails to apply in the English data used here. In a wider sense, though, when it does work, it picks out *bananas* and *stupid* as the heads of their respective phrases. So we have a series of criteria (of which (a)–(e) are symptomatic) which agree in determining headedness with the phrase.

If we try to apply these criteria to morphological examples, though, we meet problems. Part of the problem is that compounds°, derivatives° and inflected forms do not seem to function the same way in respect of these criteria. The second is that not all derivatives seem to function the same way in respect of these criteria. The third is the criteria do not agree in picking out a head in morphology as they do in syntax.

Consider, for instance, the hyponymy criterion (c). For a compound word like *windmill*, this criterion easily picks out the second element as the head. For a derivative like *unhappy*, it is not clear what it picks out. *Unhappy* is not a hyponym° of *happy*, it is its antonym, and neither is *unhappy* obviously a hyponym of *un-*. With a word like *duckling*, we might claim either that a *duckling* is a kind of *duck* (first element is the head), or that *duckling* is a kind of small entity (second element is the head). With an inflected form like *walked*, it seems to make more sense to say that *walked* is a specification of WALK (but note that we have changed from word-form° to lexeme°, which might be considered to be cheating) than that *walked* is a hyponym of 'past tense'.

The obligatoriness criterion fares little better. For *windmill* it is clear that it picks out *mill* as the head. For any instance of affixation, it seems reasonable to say that the base is obligatory, because you cannot have a word without a base, but you can have a word without an affix. With *unhappy* and *duckling*, this works brilliantly, but with *friendly* it is less successful because although we must have a base to have a word, in context we will need an adjective where we have *friendly*, and *friend* is not an adjective: we cannot substitute *friend* for *friendly* in *She seems very friendly*. With inflection, the problems are increased again, because it was argued above (Section 3.4.1) that inflection is obligatory, and we seem to have a clash between two understandings of obligatoriness. We cannot have an inflection with no lexeme to inflect, but we cannot use the lexeme in context without the inflection.

Criterion (d) goes some way to sorting out the problem. *Mill* has the same distribution as *windmill* (strictly, a rather wider one, since *mill* can occur in *millpond*, but not *windmill*, but in most places there is a match).

Happy has the same distribution as *unhappy*, *duck* has the same distribution as *duckling*, but no element in *friendly* has the same distribution as *friendly*. With an inflected form like *walked*, no element has the same distribution as the whole word.

These results are so problematic, and so confusing, and so difficult to apply, that most people who talk about a head in morphology restrict themselves to criterion (a), which they then elaborate slightly. In a compound like *blackbird*, the compound is a noun because the second element in it is a noun. If, instead of looking at English, we look instead at a language like German, then *Schwarzmarkt* 'black market' is masculine because *Markt* 'market' is a masculine noun, and the plural of *Schwarzmarkt* is *Schwarzmärkte* because the plural of *Markt* is *Märkte*. That is, the second element determines not only the word-class° of the compound°, but also the gender° class and the inflection class. This is harder to see in English than in German, but the plural of *dormouse* is *dormice* because the plural of MOUSE is *mice* (and many speakers make the plural of *mongoose mongeese*, even though there is no morpheme {goose} in *mongoose*).

If we apply the same principle to derivational morphology, then *happy* determines the word-class of *unhappy*, it is hard to tell what determines the word-class of *duckling* (in the German equivalent *Entchen* 'duckling' it is the suffix which determines gender, though in Spanish *patito* 'duckling' it is the base, meaning 'duck'), and it is *-ly* which makes *friendly* an adjective. In German, a word like *Erfahrung* 'experience' is feminine because the suffix *-ung* marks it as being feminine. Some authorities have generalised this as the Righthand-Head Rule°, with the claim that the head of a word is always the rightmost element in the word. Even in English there are a few examples, all of them derived verbs, which call this generalisation into question. These are words like *bewitch*, *de-ice*, *dismember*, *enrich*, *unhorse*, all of which are verbs despite the word-class° of the second (right-hand) element in them. These words really are a puzzle, and some authorities go so far as to postulate a zero-suffix which makes these words verbs in order to avoid exceptions to the Righthand-Head Rule. If we look more widely across languages, there are many instances of left-headed words, such as the French *poisson scie* ('fish saw = swordfish'), which is a kind of *poisson*, not a kind of *scie*.

But the greatest difficulty with the Righthand-Head Rule arises with inflection. The whole point about inflectional morphology is that it does not cause a change of word-class°, so if we take a form like *walked*, it would seem to be *walk* which makes it a verb, not *-ed*. In English, this is particularly true since there is a word-form *walk* which is a noun, as well. We might argue that it is only because *walk* is a verb that we are able to add the suffix *-ed* at all. On the other hand, if we go back to the notion of a neutral lexical entry (see Section 3.4.1), then adding the inflection is an overt sign that the form emerging is a verb, and so we might want to say that it is the inflection which makes it a verb. The argument may be genuinely insoluble, because it may depend upon other assumptions about the form of the grammar. If we assume that *walk* is the base of the verb, and we deduce that in a sentence like *I walk the dog every morning* it is present tense because it is not marked as past tense, then we want to say that *walk* is a verb and *-ed* does not need to be specifically marked as a verb. If, on the other hand, and in line with the kind of word-based morphology discussed in Chapter 3, we want to say that in *I walk the dog every morning, walk* is the word-form which realises° the first person singular of the present tense of the verb WALK, then the word-class° is defined by the lexeme° and not by any of the phonological material which makes up the word-form, and it may be reasonable to claim that *-ed* realises, among other things, the verbal nature of the entire word. In a strict syntax of words approach, however, such an argument does not seem to be available, since the items in the syntax are explicitly the morphs.

An alternative view is that the tense marks a 'relativised head'; it does not mark the word-class°, but it marks the tensedness of the word in the word-class. This gives rise to two problems: it is a completely new reading of the notion of head, one which allows multiple heads in the same word; the features which otherwise are supposed to be inherent in a head are not found in such a relativised head. Neither does the idea of a relativised head explain why we should not take the *un-* in *unhappy* and say that it is a relativised head because it marks the adjective as being negative.

The notion of head works extremely well in compounds. In English, we might even go so far as to say that when we have items like *the letter L, the number nine, a model T* these cannot be compounds because they are not right-headed (Bauer et al. 2013). There are still forms like *passer-by,* and so on which seem to be left-headed, but they may not be compounds, either, but nominalisations° of the phrasal verb *to pass by,* and so on. In other languages, compounds are not necessarily consistent in their headedness: Vietnamese appears to have left- and right-headed compounds, for example. But for a large class of compounds, and even in a language like Vietnamese, the notion of head seems valuable. With derivation°, matters are less clear, but in the majority of cases the criterion of word-class can be valuable and lead to useful insights (as in Lieber 1992). Where inflection° is concerned, the whole notion is called into question, and it is not clear how headedness should work. If word syntax concerned itself solely with the creation of structure within lexemes, and left inflection to a word grammar, then the notion of head might indeed be coherent; it is not clear that such an approach is theoretically coherent.

But in any case, the value of headedness in morphology is not really the important point. If headedness is used in morphology because the notion is taken from syntax, and the intention is to exploit the parallels between syntax and morphology, then using the same label 'head' at both levels seems very misleading. Whatever a head is in morphology, or however it can be defined, it does not seem to be true that it is the same notion that is used in syntax, because the criteria used to define 'head' are so different at the two levels.

4.4 Morphotactics

In any theory which sees the structure of words as a sequence of smaller elements, the question arises as to how these elements are ordered. In word-based morphology, as outlined in Chapter 3, this is dealt with by the rules constructing phonological structure, but the elements strung together by the phonology have, in principle, no morphological value, the morphological status belongs purely to the complete word. In a syntax of words approach, ordering is critical.

Even if we take a simple example such as *equalise*, where it is clear that the suffix *-ise* is added to the base *equal*, we can ask whether the base chooses the suffix or the suffix chooses the base. We can also ask whether there are any properties of the base or the suffix which allow the sequence *equalise*, but do not allow *equalify* or *equalen*. These properties will presumably include word-class°, but we can still ask whether the suffix is added to a word of a particular word-class, or whether a word of a particular word-class allows *-ise* affixation. When we find longer sequences of morphs, as in *sensationalism* or *hopelessness* or French *dorm-i-ons* 'sleep-TENSE.MARKER-1PL we were sleeping', the questions become proportionally more complex. One of the questions we might then ask is whether there is a maximum length in affixes for a word. Multiple answers to these problems have been provided in the literature – both specifically for English, and more generally – but, as we might expect, there is no overall agreement.

The question of whether the base chooses the affix or the affix chooses the base is of interest in the light of the discussion of headedness in Section 4.3. Other things being equal, we might expect the head to choose what goes with it, and so the conclusion here might feed back into that discussion.

In the specific case of *-ise* versus *-ify*, Plag (1999) argues in detail that the two suffixes are more or less in complementary distribution° depending on the phonology° of the base. (The phonology is complex, but is largely determined by the overall stress-pattern of the word once the suffix has been added.) Thus we find distributions like those in (3).

(3)	diversify	*diversise
	humidify	*humidise
	simplify	*simpleise
	*Italianify	Italianise
	*legalify	legalise
	*radicalify	radicalise

In a few places, the phonology of the base allows either: a disyllabic base ending in an unstressed /i/, for instance, gives us *glorify*, *nazify* but *Disneyise* and *Dolbyise* (perhaps *Disneyfy* would not raise eyebrows in its spoken form, but it provides problems for the orthographic° system). Sometimes, though, the form of the base° is altered to allow the appropriate phonological form: we get *liquefy* but *liquidise*, and *humidify* has the stress on the second syllable rather than the first to allow *-ify* to be added. So, which chooses which? If we never changed the phonology of the base, we might be able to argue either way, but if the phonology of the base is changed to allow an affix to appear, it seems as though the affix is determining the form of the base, and the affix is the head.

Now consider the following nominalisations°, all listed from Hornby (2000): *conference*, *conferment*, *deference*, *deferment*, *deferral*, *inference*, *preference*, *preferment*, *reference*, *referral*, *transfer*, *transference*. Clearly, the precise forms we have in current English owe a great deal to historical accident, and some of these nominalisations have no doubt been created to mark a semantic difference from another nominalisation from the same base. Nonetheless, there is no logic to these nominalisations: *-ence* is found everywhere, but there is no obvious logic to which other forms arise. Notably, there does not appear to be any consistent semantic factor influencing the choice of nominalisation. In this example, it looks as though the base has chosen the nominalisation rather than the contrary.

The real difficulty in this area is that most of the evidence seems to be capable of being interpreted in either direction. Consider the evidence provided by unique morphs°, for instance. At first glance, it seems easier to say of *-ric* that it attaches only to *bishop* than to say of *bishop* that one of the things it may attach to is *-ric*. But either formulation will give the appropriate outcome. Or consider the fact that some affixes, such as *-ship*, are very rarely found followed by any other affix (Bauer et al. 2013 cite one unusual example). This might be interpreted as meaning that affixes choose what can occur to their right. However, it might also be analysed as indicating that no other affix is marked as attaching to *-ship*.

The same problem affects what I consider to be the best argument: if affixation is productive, this can be accounted for by allowing affixes to choose their bases and having a very wide set of possibilities for the base (perhaps, for example, any noun); if bases choose their affixes, then there is no way to determine what affixes could be added to a newly invented base. In essence, this is an argument from economy, and as has already been said, economy does not necessarily match psychological reality, and bases could choose their affixes not on the basis of having a list of possible affixes which can co-occur with them, but on the basis of some form of analogical patterning based on phonological structure.

Overall, then, we can note co-occurrence, but it is much harder to prove direction of influence, and so there is no solid argument for headedness to be obtained from this evidence.

An alternative approach is to divide affixes into a number of classes that are ordered in respect of each other. For English, most authorities deal in two classes, though some prefer three (treating inflectional affixes as the third class). Although there are various correlates with the two classes of affix, the original distinction is between native° and non-native° (sometimes equivalently called 'learned' or 'Latinate') affixes. When foreign words are absorbed into English, it happens piecemeal, and it is only after the event that speakers start to see the patterns in the foreign words (providing enough of them are borrowed). Accordingly, foreign words are borrowed with their foreign affixes attached, but speakers can attach native affixes to those borrowed words, just as they can attach them to native words. The result is that native affixes may attach to bases on their own, or they may attach outside (further from the root° than) non-native affixes; non-native affixes can occur on their own, but not outside native suffixes. Inflectional affixes are native, but attach outside all derivational affixes (see Section 3.3). Thus we can have *personality* (*-al* and *-ity* are both non-native), *mannishness* or *womanliness* (*-ish*, *-ly* and *-ness* are all native), even *personalness* (with native *-ness* further from the root, *person*, than the non-native *-al*), but we cannot have **personishity*, **womanlity*, with native *-ish* or *-ly* closer to the root than non-native *-ity*.

There are two main problems with such approaches. The first is that the observations on which they are based are incomplete: there are many cases of native inside non-native in precisely the way that is predicted not to occur: *resharpenable*, *computerese*, *blenderise*, *Yiddishist*, *rhymsterette* (for more examples and discussion, see Bauer et al. 2013: ch. 27). The second is that even if the observations were accurate, they would need to be complemented with another set of rules to establish the order between the various native affixes or the various non-native affixes. If this second set of rules is required anyway, it is not clear that we need the division into native and non-native to support it.

A third way of looking at affix ordering is in terms of semantics. Consider a word like *equalises*. We start with the root°, *equal*, and to that we add *-ise*. The suffix adds its own meaning – perhaps 'cause to be ~', where the swung dash represents the meaning of the base°, *equal*. If we make the base more complex, as in *regionalise*, the meaning is still 'cause to be regional'; that is, the meaning of *-ise* influences the entire base, not just the last element in the base. In technical terminology, *-ise* has scope° over all of *equal*, and *regional*. Similarly, the final /ɪz/ makes all of *equalise* third person singular present tense. Again, the affix has scope over everything to which it has been added. As we saw at the start of this chapter, we use this semantic information to determine the tree structure of a word. Now we can look at it from another angle and say that any affix has scope over the entire base to which it is added, and the order of the affixes is thus determined by what has scope over what.

A related approach sees ordering as being largely determined by the twin factors of relevance and lexical generality. The degree of relevance° of an affix is defined by the amount of semantic difference it makes to the base, while lexical generality° is defined in terms of the number of different words the affix (and its meaning) can be applied to. The more relevant some meaning is, the more likely it is to be shown by the use of completely separate lexemes, or by derivation; that is, the more likely it is to be marked on or close to the root. The more lexically general some meaning is, the more likely it is to be marked inflectionally, that is, peripherally in the word-form. Consider sex-marking in English. It is obviously relevant, because we have lots of words where we use a different lexeme° for the female and the male (consider *king, queen*; *husband, wife*; *dog, bitch*; *drake, duck*; *stallion, mare*; and so on). We can also mark it morphologically (in English this almost always means marking the female, but note *widower*): *countess, priestess, hostess, actress, tigress, pantheress*. While this suffix is relevant, it is not lexically general. Not only does it apply only to animals, it applies only to those whose sex is important to humans: we would not expect *mousess, frogess, snakess, flyess* (though they would no doubt be interpretable in context). On the other hand, plurality is lexically general – it can apply to huge numbers of nouns, perhaps most of them – but it does not affect the semantic status of any of them particularly strongly. We would therefore expect to find plurality marked further from the root than sex, which, of course, is what we find in *lionesses*, and the like.

Finally in this overview of affix ordering, we can consider an approach based on form. Consider a word like *amendment.* It is clear that there must be a boundary of some kind between the /d/ and the /m/, because no monomorphemic° element of English contains the cluster /dm/. On the other hand, although there is a boundary in *profitability* between the /t/ and the /ɪ/ (and again between the /l/ and the /ɪ/), this boundary is not as clear, since many monomorphemic elements can contain the sequences /tɪ/and /lɪ/: consider *attic* and *solid*, for example. Thus the affix in *amendment* is phonologically more parsable than the affixes in *profitability* are. There is also a semantic side to parsability: the sequence *-ness* /nɪs/ at the end of word is almost always a suffix and nearly always has the same meaning ('state of being ~'), and so the speaker/listener can rely on being able to attach a meaning to the form; on the other hand, the sequence *-e(r)* /ə(r)/ while often associated with one of several meanings ('comparative', 'agent', 'instrument', 'location', 'inhabitant of', etc.) is also frequently not a suffix at all, as in *after*, *aster*, *barter*, *Easter*, *October*, *plaster*, *sinister*, *sister*, *Winchester*, *youngster*, and so on. In general terms, we would expect to find more parsable affixes further from the root than less parsable affixes. In *raffishness*, *-ness* is more phonologically parsable than *-ish*, because of the /ʃn/ at the boundary; in *friendliness*, *-ness* is more semantically parsable than *-ly*, whose main meaning is adverbial. Somehow the two sides of parsability have to be integrated, and either a calculation has to be made in each word, or some kind of average level of parsability has to be determined for any affix if this is to be applied in any practical sense; this does not mean that it cannot be a psychologically appropriate way of determining order.

At the end of all this, we do not have a nice clear way of determining affix order, although any of the points that have been considered might play some kind of role to a greater or lesser degree. It is not that the problem is clearly insoluble, but rather that there are so many factors involved that it is hard to see how they might work together to give a good solution. What is clear, though, is that any solution that employs the kinds of factors that have been considered here is going to be complex.

4.5 Conclusion

Two of the main corollaries of a word syntax approach to morphology, headedness and affix ordering, have turned out to be rather more complicated than we might have envisaged. For a word-syntax approach to be viable, it really needs to have answers to these two fundamental topics. The fact that a morphology based on a notion of headedness whose definition is reliant almost solely on word-class° can be made to function well and provide some insights (as in Lieber 1992) is of considerable interest, but it does not really solve the problem of why this is supposed to be a parallel with syntax, a part of a larger structural analogy°. It might be possible to have a syntax without any linearisation involved (such matters have often been ignored in syntactic studies, and are assumed to be clear), but a large part of syntax is precisely putting the elements in the right order, and syntactic typologies show that the relative ordering of elements is important and not random. As someone who has often taken an implicit (if not explicit) syntax of words view of morphology, I would not wish to discard this view of morphology out of hand. It seems clear, however, that there are gaps to be filled in the theory.

Notes and comments

While an analysis of affixation based on scope° may work well for English and other Indo-European languages, it is generally assumed not to work in languages with templatic morphology. In languages with templatic morphology, there are a number of slots in every paradigm°, and in each slot there are a number of forms which may occur in a paradigmatic relationship with each other. The form which occurs and the slot in which it occurs together produce a meaning, sometimes in conjunction with other forms in other slots in the paradigm. For a discussion, see Stump (1997).

Reading

On the syntax of words in general, see Selkirk (1982), Toman (1998) and Lieber (1992).

On the question of compounds and whether we can distinguish them from syntactic constructions, there is quite an extensive literature. Although the arguments were going on for a long time before these papers, the interested reader is directed to Bauer (1998b) and the response in Giegerich (2004), and also to Bell (2011).

On headedness, see Bauer (1990) and Lieber (1992), which take contrasting approaches to the problem and accordingly come to different conclusions. On adding a zero-suffix to words like *de-ice*, see Nakano (2011). On relativised heads, see Di Sciullo and Williams (1987).

On scope driving the order of affixation, see Rice (2000). On relevance and lexical generality, see Bybee (1985).

On parsability of affixes, see Hay (2003).

On whether bases select affixes or vice versa, see Giegerich (1999). This is also a good source on the division of affixes into native and non-native, for which see also Kiparsky (1982) and Bauer et al. (2013).

Discussion questions

Some suggested answers to these questions can be found in the Answers to Discussion Questions at edinburghuniversitypress.com/rethinkingmorphology

1. *Booklet*, *duckling*, *minicar* and *roomette* all denote something that is smaller than the norm. *Supermarket*, *hypermarket*, *maxicoat* and *megabit* all denote something that is bigger than the norm (literally or figuratively). What are the heads in these constructions? Are prefixed items different from suffixed items? Are diminutives different from augmentatives? Justify your conclusions.
2. There is a set of compounds in English which are sometimes called 'tautological compounds°'. Examples are given below. Are these compounds left-headed or right-headed? Are they all the same? How do you determine this?

   (a) canary bird
   (b) cod fish
   (c) collie dog
   (d) oak tree
   (e) pathway
   (f) pine tree
   (g) tuna fish
   (h) vegetable marrow
   (i) widow woman

   For some discussion of tautological compounds, see Benczes (2014).
3. There are words with sequences of derivational suffixes in English like *sensationalise*, *realisation*, *organisational*. Can the order of the affixes be predicted by any of the methods suggested in the chapter? Are there any other principles which might apply? Can you find any other sequences of three suffixes in English? Do the same principles apply to them?
4. Is there any reason to suggestion that *-al* chooses to be added to *-ation*, or that *-ation* chooses *-al* to be added to it in words like *informational*?

5 The phonological correlates of concatenation

5.1 Introduction

The moment we put two linguistic items together in the chain of speech, there is the possibility that one will affect the other in terms of their pronunciation. Sometimes the effect is relatively minor. For example, some people might pronounce *at all* differently from *a tall*, others may pronounce them the same way. For those that pronounce them the same way, the /t/, which lexically is at the end of *at*, has somehow been analysed by the speaker as being phonologically at the beginning of *all*, rather than at the end of *at*. We still have a /t/, but it is a phonetically different version of /t/, depending on where it is seen to belong in the word or the syllable. A more complex example is provided by the word *handbag*. It is possible to say this so that the elements *hand* and *bag* are phonetically very clear, and rather like the pronunciation of each of the elements in isolation. But most of the time, most of us pronounce it as if it were *hambag*. If the only elements we deal with are words, then we need to describe the phenomena that can or do occur when words are placed next to each other. If we also have morphemes° as separate elements, we also need to describe what happens when they are placed together, and any description involves putting the changes that are observed into some kind of theoretical framework. These theoretical frameworks also make assumptions about how phonology interacts with morphology.

Since this book deals primarily with morphology rather than phonology°, it does not seem appropriate to spend a great deal of time discussing different phonological theories, and considering their relative strengths and weaknesses. The focus of this chapter will thus be on the phenomena which phonological and morphological theories have to deal with, individually or in tandem. Nevertheless, we can start by indicating just some of the ways in which the interaction may be interpreted from a theoretical angle, to make the point that the morphological data are often open to varying phonological (and, indeed, also morphological) interpretations.

Consider a simple example, similar to one that has already been discussed. In the words *intolerant*, *indecisive* and *inoperative*, there is a prefix *in-* which has the effect of negating the adjective in the base. In the words *immoral*, *imperfect* and *impossible* there is a corresponding prefix *im-* with the same function. (By historical accident, there is no adjective beginning with *b-* that is regularly negated in this way; we can perhaps imagine that if *bodacious* were negated using one of these prefixes, we would find *imbodacious*.) Given such a situation, we can ask the following questions:

- Are *in-* and *im-* just separate items that happen to appear in different environments (this is the IA° solution, discussed in the Notes and comments section of Chapter 2)?
- Is there a basic form *in-* which changes into *im-* under certain circumstances? If so, does this imply two different kinds of /n/, one that changes into /m/ and another, in a word like *not*, that does not? If this is the case, it is not clear why there would be an established form *enmesh*.
- Is there a basic form, which is neither *in-* nor *im-*, whose last segment has no place of articulation defined for it? If this is the case, we need to explain how the form of the prefix is specified in *inoperative*, where place of articulation does not come from the next sound.
- If there is a basic form, is the choice of actually attested form driven by some kind of rule making a change to the form of the prefix, or does the grammar choose between possible forms on the basis of some other kind of information? More generally, does the grammar choose between alternative forms, or specify an outcome, which must apply in a given set of circumstances?
- If there is a choice between /m/ and /n/ in any way, is it restricted by some generalisable feature° either of the prefix° or of the base°? If there are such classes defined by these features, are they classes of bases, affixes, both, or of all words, whether morphologically complex or not? (Such features might include phonological shape and/or morphological class and/or lexical° marking.) If this is the case, *en-* might belong to a different class from *in-*, or *operative* might belong to a different class from *mesh*. (For one approach to different classes of affix, see the discussion of native° and non-native° in Section 4.4.)
- Is it possible for there to be individual exceptions to general rules affecting the structure of words of this nature, and if so, how does

that work? If this is the case, we need to explain why *enmew* would work like *enmesh* and not like *emmarble*.

If we consider this list of questions, some of them seem to be more morphological in nature than others. If something happens to particular affixes, adjacent to particular affixes, or in particular morphological classes, then morphology must be implicated somehow in the process. Morphology clearly allows for exceptions (otherwise we cannot explain why the verb BE has past tense forms *was* and *were*, where other verbs have only one form in the past). It may be the case that phonology does not have exceptions which affect particular lexemes° in this way. This means that while some of the statements we need to make about what happens when morphemes° are brought together in sequences are purely phonological, some of them involve both phonology and morphology interacting with each other. In considering the various phenomena that we can observe, no distinction will be drawn here between phenomena with different degrees of morphological involvement. A more nuanced classification of such phenomena would clearly be possible.

The area of language which deals with such facts is called 'morphophonology°' or, in a rather more old-fashioned terminology, 'morphophonemics°'. There are various processes to be considered under such an approach to morphophonology. Not only do segments have to be modified, they have to be inserted and deleted. It is worth making the point that these morphophonological processes are language-specific. What applies in English does not necessarily apply in another language, even if it seems to be a perfectly natural process.

5.2 Deletion of phonological material

As with most of these processes, the ultimate aim of deletion processes can be seen as making the surface word as regular in structure as possible. Where deletion is concerned, this may be a matter of adjusting the length of the word or removing sequences of sounds which are difficult to pronounce. Two types of deletion will be considered here: haplology° and truncation°.

5.2.1 Haplology

Haplology° refers to the deletion of a sound adjacent to or close to a similar sound. Consider the case of the genitive° plural in English. In regular instances, the plural is marked with an *-s* suffix (variously pronounced), and the genitive is also marked with an *-s* suffix. We see that the genitive is marked in the plural in cases such as *men's*, where the plural of *man* is irregular and so does not end in an *-s* suffix. So what happens when we want to mark the genitive plural of regular nouns? We would expect to find a sequence of *-s-s*, but that is not pronounceable in English. What happens elsewhere in the language is that a vowel is inserted to keep the two stridents° apart; this happens, for instance, in *fleeces* /fliːsɪz/. But what happens in the genitive plural is that the sequence of two /s/ sounds is reduced to one, and we get, for instance, *girls'* /gɜːlz/. In written English, the difference between the plural and the genitive plural is shown by the use of the apostrophe, but there is no difference in spoken English between *It's the girls* and *It's the girls'*.

A slightly more complex example is provided by adverbs derived from adjectives that end in *-ly* (/lɪ/). You can find words like *sillily* in dictionaries, but you will probably find that most speakers avoid them (and the spelling checker on my computer does not like this one). You are less likely to find an adverb from *daily* in a dictionary, and people sometimes use the form *daily* as an adverb: *New stock arriving daily!* In such cases, you might say that the adverb *daily* arises by haplology from the expected form *dailily*.

As a final example, consider *morphophonology* itself, which is sometimes called 'morphonology', with haplology.

5.2.2 Truncation

Truncation° is the predictable deletion of material from the end of an element. Consider, for instance, the word *Chinese*. We can assume that this is derived from *China*, but the final *-a* of the base is deleted in the derivative, which has the effect of avoiding a sequence of two vowels (something which English allows over morpheme boundaries, as in *being* and *doing*, but which is relatively unusual). We find the same truncation in *Burmese* and *Maltese*. This particular pattern of truncation is not widespread (these may be the only examples), but it illustrates the general notion. A more widespread pattern is illustrated in (1). Here *-ate* is deleted before *-able*. It is not necessarily obvious whether this is a purely phonological matter, or whether it involves specifically the deletion of an affix. Note that even here, the process is not entirely automatic: *educatable* is also found.

(1)	communicate	communicable
	demonstrate	demonstrable

educate	educable
isolate	isolable
navigate	navigable
regulate	regulable

The suffix -*ate* is also frequently deleted before -*ee*, as in *designee* from *designate.*

There are those who deny the existence of truncation. They say that in examples like those in (1), nothing is deleted, the -*able* affixation just adds something to a base° which is not a word. If there is no deletion, then the places where no -*ate* suffix is added need to be spelt out in some other manner.

5.3 Addition of phonological material

In Turkish, the genitive° ending for nouns ending in a consonant is -*in*, as in *elin* 'of the hand' from *el* 'hand', *denizin* 'of the sea' from *deniz* 'sea'. When the noun ends in a vowel, in contrast, an extra -*n*- is added, as in *gecenin* 'of the night' from *gece* 'night', *geminin* 'of the ship' from *gemi* 'ship'. We could see this as an allomorph° of the genitive appearing after a vowel, or as a process of consonant insertion, keeping two vowels apart.

We find similar phenomena in English, but not as consistently. Consider the varied instances of insertion in (2).

(2)	cell	cellular
	Congo	Congolese
	drama	dramatic
	Peru	Peruvian
	Plato	Platonic
	recur	recursion
	witty	witticism

In some instances, it is clear that the inserted material belongs closely with either the base° or with the suffix°. In *Platonic*, for instance, the -*n*- belongs with the base, because it also occurs in *Platonist, Platonism, Platonise.* In *professorial*, the -*i*- seems to belong closely with the suffix, because the -*i*- occurs in many instances with a range of bases (e.g. *equinoctial, financial, ministerial*), and is not consistently conditioned by bases that end in -*or* (consider *doctoral, electoral, pastoral* alongside *conspiratorial, dictatorial, tutorial*). These extra pieces of form can be termed 'extenders°' (Bauer et al. 2013: 16): they extend the base or the affix.

5.4 The modification of phonological material

We started this chapter with an example where the prefixes *in-* and *im-* are synonymous° and occur in different environments which are predictable. Such cases are very often viewed as changes to the form of the relevant morph, and the dynamic metaphor is widespread in linguistics. But as we saw in Section 5.1, that is not the only way in which such patterns can be envisaged. There are multiple instances of this general pattern, but they are not all equivalent, because there are variable motivations for the different forms. Four rather different instances will be treated below: assimilation, remnants of former phonological processes, simplification and structure optimisation.

5.4.1 Assimilation

Assimilation is often viewed as a phonological process, and so it is here that the processual terminology is hardest to avoid. In phonological assimilation, it is usually said, one segment becomes more like another, usually adjacent, segment, most often in order to facilitate articulation. In morphology, arguably, we deal with the outcome of assimilatory processes, in that we find allomorphs° whose form has historically been determined by assimilation. The example of *im-* before a bilabial and *in-* elsewhere is thus based on assimilation. The case of the English regular plural marker being /s/ after a non-strident° voiceless° consonant (as in *cuffs*, *plates*) and /z/ after any voiced° non-strident (as in *lads*, *things*, *pizzas*) is another case. To the extent that we want to view such a pattern as a process, we assume that /z/ is the basic form because it is the most widespread form, the 'elsewhere°' form, the form we find when there are no specific requirements to change it.

5.4.2 Remnants of historical processes

In some instances, the process of assimilation, or any other process, is no longer productive° in modern English, and what we see are the results of a process which once affected the relevant words. Consider the examples in (3) from English.

(3)	divide	division
	erode	erosion
	erupt	eruption
	president	presidential
	radiate	radiation

In (3) we see that in the first column we have /t/ or /d/ in word-final position, and in the second column we have the corresponding post-alveolar fricative (/ʃ/ or /ʒ/) before the letter <i>. The letter <i> is not pronounced. This is not a current English rule. If it were, we would expect *tidier* to be pronounced /taɪʒə/, which is not what happens. We can, with some difficulty, formulate this as a set of phonological rules, some of which may have wider application in English. The bottom line, though, is that this is not a rule of English at all; it is the remnant of a rule in French. The process is complex, and we see only the final stage. We cannot really explain it in terms of English.

Another similar case in English is the case of so-called ‘velar softening°’. In velar softening, a word-final /k/ is replaced by a /s/ before certain affixes, including *-ity* and *-ism*, as in *opacity* and *romanticism* (*romanti/k/* becomes *romanti/s/ism*). Here, the presence of specific affixes is an important part of the environment or the change.

In historical terms, the relationship between *foot* and *feet* is similar. At one stage in the history of English the plural of *foot* had a suffix *-iz*, and the /i/ vowel in the suffix affected the vowel in the base°, making it more /i/-like. This process is called ‘umlaut°’. With the subsequent loss of the suffix, the motivation for this change is now completely lost, and only the morphological alternation remains. This example shows how something that was once a phonological relationship has changed over time to being a morphological relationship.

5.4.3 Cluster simplification

English does not allow a cluster of /mn/ in the same syllable. At the beginning of a word like *mnemonic*, <mn> is pronounced /n/. Sometimes, though, when <mn> occurs between vowel sounds, it is pronounced /mn/, and sometimes it is pronounced simply as /m/ (which is also how it is pronounced at the end of a word). So we find examples like those in (4), where the following vowel sound is part of a suffix: in (4a) we see what happens with /mn/, and in (4b) what happens with /ŋg/, which is (except in British accents of places like Lancashire and Birmingham) rather similar.

(4)	(a)	/m/	/mn/ + V	/m/ + V
		autumn	autumnal	
		condemn	condemnable	condemning
		damn	damnable	damning
		column	columnal	columned
			columnist	columnist

(b) /ŋ/	/ŋg/ + V	/ŋ/ + V
sing	finger	singer
long	longer ('more long')	longer ('one who longs')
hang	anger	hangar

Here there is a theoretical problem in determining just what factors lead to cluster simplification, a problem which is made more difficult by the fact that some words allow for either pronunciation, but the observation of cluster simplification accompanying some suffixation is robust.

5.4.4 Structure optimisation

In Swahili, the noun-class marker *u-* is replaced by *w-* before a vowel, so that we get the forms illustrated in (5).

(5)
utoto	'childhood'
ufalme	'kingdom'
uzuri	'beauty'
ubaya	'evil'
wema	'goodness'
wingi	'plenitude'

The sounds /u/ and /w/ are virtually identical in phonetic terms (though much less so in modern English), but differ phonologically in their status as consonants or vowels. The pattern outlined in (5) leads to an alternation between consonants and vowels rather than a sequence of vowels, and this is generally considered to be an easier structure to process.

5.5 Wider phonological change

Many of the examples that have been discussed so far have the result of leading to allomorphs° of the bases° or of the affixes°. Such a view, of course, assumes a morpheme-based approach to morphology, and makes little sense in a word-based morphology setting. The types of allomorphy that have been illustrated so far, however, do not exhaust the ways in which allomorphy can be created. In no particular order, some others are listed here.

The examples in (6) illustrate stress-change.

(6)
(a)	Japan	Japanese
(b)	motive	motivation
(c)	parent	parental

(d) telepath telepathic
(e) potent impotent

The stress in these words sometimes moves from the base° to the affix° (6a, b, e), sometimes to another syllable in the base (6c, d), the precise position here often seen as being determined by the affix.

Frequently stress-change leads to vowel reduction; in English this is most often a change to /ə/.

(7) eleph/ə/nt eleph/æ/ntine
p/eə/rent p/ə/rental
pref/ɜː/ pref/ə/rable
telep/æ/th telep/ə/thy

There are instances where there is a change in vowel quality without any reduction: this can be termed 'vowel alternation°' or 'apophony°'. Several distinguishable types are included in (8).

(8) conc/iː/ve conc/e/ption
div/aɪ/n div/ɪ/nity
gl/ɑː/ss gl/eɪ/zier
l/ɔː/ l/ɔɪ/yer
n/eɪ/tion n/æ/tional

Sometimes the vowels which alternate in such cases appear to be idiosyncratic, as perhaps in *G/ɔː/l* and *G/æ/llic*, some of them are relatively predictable over large numbers of words. For example, the alternation between /iː/ and /e/ occurs in free variation° in words like *economic*, *Kenya*, *Megan*, *oestrus*, *plenary*, *scenic*, where they simply provide alternative pronunciations of the words. But the same alternation is tied up with morphology in pairs such as *compete/competitive*, *convene/convention*, *deep/depth*, *obscene/obscenity*, *serene/serenity*, *thief/theft*, and so on.

Sometimes when we expect two identical consonants over a morpheme boundary, we find a single one instead. This is called 'degemination°'. Degemination is not ubiquitous in English: *soulless* and *brazenness* retain geminate consonants (/ll/ and /nn/ respectively), but the examples in (9) probably do not. According to Upton et al. (2001), there is more degemination in US English than in British English.

(9) eighteen
fully
really
surreal

As was mentioned in Section 2.2.6, there are several processes which can, on their own, mark morphological status. In principle, these can be easily added to an Item and Process° grammar. For example, the process which shows a vowel change between *foot* and *feet*, discussed above, is much the same as the kind of process illustrated in (8), but those in (8) have some affix or equivalent to mark the change as well as the vowel change. In one case the environment for the change might be the presence of the extra affix, in the other, the environment is the presence of the relevant category (plural, in the instance of *feet*).

5.6 Conclusion

Phonology is tightly interwoven with morphology. Even in the case of affixation, extra phonological material represents extra meaning. In other cases, changes to the phonological string may represent that extra meaning, or may be additional correlates to the morphological change. Sometimes phonological change is no different from that found when words are placed together by syntactic rules; very often the phonology that affects morphological concatenation is different from that which affects syntactic concatenation. In either case, the study of morphology requires some consideration of the way in which phonology is exploited in morphological contexts.

Notes and comments

One important question about phonology remains unanswered in this chapter: which phonological processes are to be determined by the phonological component (possibly in interaction with the morphological component), and which are simply lexical facts which have to be learned? Is the fact that /l/ is inserted between base and affix in *Congolese* a phonological fact, or is it simply a lexical fact? Although I have treated all insertion as being the same here, I believe that this particular rule of consonant insertion is a purely lexical fact, and nothing to do with phonology. My position on this was set out as early as Bauer (1978).

Reading

On Item and Process morphology, see Hockett ([1954] 1957). There are many phonology textbooks from the late twentieth century which provide an introduction to the phonology of the kinds of process discussed here, but they are out of date. On phonological processes in

English morphology, see Bauer et al. (2013: ch. 9). The whole question of the different kinds of morphophonology, ignored here, is dealt with by Dressler (1985).

Discussion questions

Some suggested answers to these questions can be found in the Answers to Discussion Questions at edinburghuniversitypress.com/rethinkingmorphology

1. In the question of *enmesh* but **enbark*, does the existence of a word like *enmity* suggest a potential answer to what the real generalisation may be?
2. If *-able* is sometimes added to something that is not a word, and the same is true of *-ee*, does the existence of words like *civilisable* and *civilisee* create a problem? What about words like *dedicatee, rotatable*?
3. In Section 5.3 it was said that the variation between *-in* and *-nin* for the Turkish genitive could be seen either as a phonological rule of insertion or as a morphological pattern of allomorphy. Is there any advantage to one or the other of these analyses? Does it make any difference to your conclusion to know that while the consonant inserted in the genitive is /n/, this is not the consonant added in other cases (elsewhere it is /j/)?
4. What are the etymological° sources of the inserted phonological material in the examples in (2)? To what extent is such insertion predictable in English? Extend the examples for each type, or look for other types of insertion.
5. The cases illustrated in (4) are similar in that they involve the simplification of clusters in certain environments, but they differ as to the environments in which the simplification is found. Are there any generalisations about the conditioning factors for these simplifications? Check your own personal answers against those given by some dictionary which provides information on pronunciation. Does the dictionary agree with you? If not, what might this imply?
6. Perhaps one of the most often heard instances of phonological deletion over morpheme boundaries in English is not represented in the spelling, and is subject to reinstatement in particularly clear forms of speech. It is the deletion of the /t/ (and perhaps the /s/) in words like *casts* (/kɑːst/ + /s/ > /kɑːsts/ > /kɑːss/ > /kɑːsˑ/ > /kɑːs/). Is this process any different in principle from the processes

discussed in the chapter? Why (not)? Would you want to make distinctions between classes of morphophonological processes? If not, why not? If so, on what basis and why? (Dressler 1985 provides some suggestions.)

7. Choose one of the vowel alternations illustrated in (8), and look for further examples of it. Do general patterns of occurrence arise?

6 The borders of morphology

6.1 Introduction

In this chapter, rather than looking at ways in which morphological structure has been dealt with from a theoretical point of view, the intention is to look at a series of phenomena which may or may not be morphological. The phenomena to be considered are all concerned in some way with the internal structure of words, but whether they are part of morphology proper is in some cases controversial, in others not controversial at all – some of these phenomena are regularly excluded from morphology, others are included. None of them, however, is part of central morphology, which I take to include affixation, conversion° and compounding. By considering these phenomena, we are considering phenomena which lie somewhere near the borders of morphology, and in order to demarcate morphology, we need to determine which of these should be included under the heading of morphology.

In this chapter, many words from Barnhart et al. (1990) are cited, and they are followed by a parenthesised capital (B), to save space in the referencing.

6.2 Meaning without form

Consider the set of words in (1).

(1) (a) dog
(b) bitch, pup, whelp
(c) dachshund, greyhound, Labrador, Newfoundland, poodle, retriever, spaniel, terrier, whippet

In (1a) we find a superordinate° term, and in (1b) and (1c) we find different sets of hyponyms° of that superordinate term. Clearly there is some kind of semantic relationship between them, and it would be simple to create some kind of analysis where they all shared a feature° such as [Species: canine]. Yet this is generally accepted as being excluded from morphology, since there is no shared form and no possible analysis into recurrent morphs°. Yet this relationship is linguistically important. Because we can say that *The dog barked/ growled/ whined/ sniffed*, and so on, we can use the same verbs with each of the hyponyms. So certain collocations are guaranteed because of the hyponymy, and this is a type of syntactic relevance (albeit not the type usually demanded in deciding whether something is or is not inflectional). We do not even have to have a superordinate term for this to hold. Consider words such as *bitch*, *cow*, *mare*, *tigress* which share values for adult, female and mammal and thus allow collocations with verbs like *give birth to* and *suckle*.

Sometimes semantic relationships without form are seen as being morphological, though. The obvious examples are things like tense, where *caught*, *fell*, *rode*, *swam*, *walked* are, at least in word-based morphology, deemed to have something in common despite the lack of form that they share. In word-based morphology, this is because the semantic content is the semantic content of a morphosyntactic feature°, and not some random piece of semantic commonality. This prioritises inflection over derivation, as is typical within word-based morphology. But even within morpheme-based morphology, many analysts would see this set of words as sharing a morpheme, although we have seen that such an analysis may cause problems (see Section 2.2.1). Even a morphemic analysis of this kind prioritises inflectional morphology and uses the paradigmatic° structure of inflectional morphology as a covert argument for morphemic structure. If there is a distinction to be drawn here, care needs to be taken in drawing it, and any comprehensive theory of morphology requires a principled statement of where the borderline between morphological semantic commonality and non-morphological semantic commonality runs.

6.3 Form without meaning

Because there is an arbitrary relationship between form° and meaning (Saussure 1916), it often happens that semantically unrelated forms share a certain amount of phonological structure. Some examples are given in (2), where we see the beginning of the word, the end of the word and the syllable and stress patterns of the word being shared.

(2) (a) plan, planet, plangent, plantain
(b) architrave, behave, deprave, engrave, knave, wave
(c) bonnet, college, mitten, mullet, solid

While such commonalities are usually taken to be no more than coincidental, there is a theory of word recognition which states that when we hear a word we narrow down what the word must be by excluding words which have incompatible initial segments (Marslen-Wilson 1987). So if we hear *plan*, at /p/ we might think that the word will be *perpendicular*, but that is excluded by the /l/, and when we hear /æ/ we can exclude *plane*, *plate*, *plight*, *plum*, and so on. Eventually, either the word is complete or we get to the point where there is only one word in our vocabularies which fits the available information, and so we do not have to pay as much attention to the ends of words. If such a theory holds, then the word *plantain* must activate the other words in (2a), even if not at a conscious level (Marslen-Wilson and Zwitserlood 1989). So there is likely to be some kind of link between them.

More importantly, though, there are ways in which this phonological similarity is exploited by speakers, in phenomena such as alliteration, assonance and rhyme.

Alliteration° was used in older English for poetic effect, and some of that still remains in the language, even if not in the same form. Not only do we find poetic use of it, in lines such as those in (3), it comes out in many fixed phrases, as illustrated in (4).

(3) By the ever-rolling river,
Swollen with the summer rain,
Threading long and leafy mazes
Dotted with unnumbered daisies;
Scaling rough and rugged passes,
Climb the hardy little lasses,
Till the bright sea-shore they gain

(W. S. Gilbert, *The Pirates of Penzance*)

(4) (a) black and blue, carry the can, cool as a cucumber, cowardy custard, dog's dinner, fair and free, fame and fortune, friend or foe, good as gold, large as life, look lively, neither fish, flesh, fowl nor good red herring, pleased as Punch, thick as thieves, where's Wally

(b) blood bank, boy band, firefly, free phone, goosegog, jungle juice, people power

The phrases in (4a) all have syntactic structure, even if they are fixed phrases, and they might not be considered to have anything to do with word structure at all. Nevertheless, the alliteration adds something to their effect, and supports their continued use. Those in (4b) look far more lexical, and to that extent are far more likely to have something to do with morphology, and the alliteration seems to have the same function that we see in (4a) of drawing attention to the structure.

Although assonance° (the repetition of vowel sounds) is less obvious in the structure of English, it is nevertheless found in many expressions, among which we can count those in (5). Again, the phonology somehow makes these expressions seem particularly apt, though we probably rarely analyse why that should be.

(5) deep freeze, flounder around, gobstopper, hot dog, long johns, Love Bug, nice as pie, plum duff, poppycock, punch-up, spend a penny, strap-hanger

Rhyme is a more familiar category, and more obvious. Again we find a range of construction types, from those where rhyme seems to be the entire reason for their existence to those where rhyme merely supports the viability of the expression. Examples are provided in (6).

(6) argy-bargy, arty-farty, back pack, blackjack, cop shop, culture vulture, double trouble, easy peasy, flower power, fuddy-duddy, fuzzy-wuzzy, gang bang, handy-dandy, happy clappy, helter-skelter, op shop, sin bin, willy-nilly, zoot suit

Finally, in (7) we find examples of expressions whose elements are linked by apophony° or vowel change. These are sometimes called 'compounds' in the literature, but that seems rather misleading since in many cases (as with some of the examples in (6)) one of the two elements, if not both, has no independent existence. Moreover, they are not obviously, as a class, right-headed (see above Section 4.3). Rather we seem to have some kind of reduplication°, sometimes with predetermined vocalism.

(7) ding-dong, dribs and drabs, fiddle-faddle, flip-flop, love you and leave you, Milly Molly Mandy, shilly-shally, slip, slap, slop, wishy-washy

Some of the examples given above can be treated as compounds, and they are most often seen as morphological constructions; but then their phonology is usually treated as being incidental. Some of the items in (6) and (7) are sometimes treated as independent types of word-formation°, but they are not obviously made up of morphemes° and might not be considered fully morphological as a result. The constructions dealt with here, then, straddle what is usually considered morphology and syntax°, but where they are considered morphological, the phonological patterning which lies at the heart of these examples is dealt with as peripheral or irrelevant. That is not to say that such processes cannot be used morphologically. Thompson ([1965] 1987: 158–67) describes Vietnamese as having emphatic markers which rhyme or alliterate; he also ([1965] 1987: 175) illustrates 'dramatics' which appear to employ apophony°.

6.4 Acronyms

We can define an acronym° as a word created from the initial letters in the words of a longer expression, and pronounced as a single word, not as a sequence of letters. Thus *UNICEF* (United Nations International Children's Emergency Fund) is an acronym, pronounced /ˈjuːnɪsef/, but *UNHCR* (United Nations High Commissioner for Refugees) is an initialism°, pronounced /ˈjuː ˈen ˈeɪʧ ˈsiː ˈɑː/, and not an acronym. The distinction is sometimes rather obscure: *faq* ('frequently asked question') is an acronym if pronounced /fæk/ but an initialism if pronounced /ˈef ˈeɪ ˈkjuː/.

In any case, the limits of acronyms are rather vague. Sometimes several letters may be taken from one word of the original, sometimes words of the original may not be represented. In German, there is a tradition of taking several letters from the beginning of each word, so that *Kripo* comes from *kriminal Polizei* 'criminal police', and such words fade into complex clippings° (see Section 6.7 for clippings). Consider, for instance, *Ameslan* (AMErican Sign LANguage), *arbo* (ARthropod BOrne) and *CANDU* (CANada Deuterium oxide-Uranium) (all B). In *CREEP* (B) (Committee to Re-Elect the President), one word provides more than one letter for the acronym, but the definite article is ignored in the acronym.

The most successful acronyms become monomorphemic° words in their own right, and cease to have any necessary connection with the underlying phrase which gave rise to them: *scuba* may not be interpreted specifically as 'self-contained underwater breathing apparatus', and *laser* may not be related to 'light amplification by stimulated emission of radiation'.

6.5 Phonaesthemes

Consider the sets of words in (8).

(8) (a) sleazy, slime, slither, slobber, slop, slush
(b) glare, gleam, glimmer, glimpse, glint, glitter, glow
(c) bump, clump, slump, thump

In each of the sets of words, there is some, perhaps rather vague, meaning which the words share and which seems to be carried by some part of the word. In (8a), the meaning might be to do with something that is tactilely unpleasant; in (8b) something to do with reflected or diffuse light; in (8c) something to do with a dull, heavy sound.

Typically, it is not clear what words fit into the series: do *slum* and *slump* belong in the first set, do *glamour* and *glass* belong in the second set, and does *dump* belong in the third, for instance? It is also the case that there are words with the same phonological sequence which almost certainly do not belong, as illustrated in (9).

(9) (a) slash, sleep, slight, slim, slumber
(b) glad, glade, glen, glide, globe
(c) chump, jump, rump, trump

In the case of *gl-* there is even a contrasting set of words where the *gl-* appears to have a different meaning, as shown in (10).

(10) glob, glo(o)p, glue, glum, glut

Furthermore, there are words which show similar meanings to those in (8) but which do not share the phonology: consider *greasy*, *radiant* and *thud*.

There is general agreement in the literature that, whatever psychological reality these word-portions may have, it is nothing to do with morphology. This is because there is no exhaustive analysis of the word: if the *sl-* at the beginning of the set in (8a) is meaningful, the same cannot be said of the *-eazy*, *-ime*, *-ither*, *-obber*, *-op* and *-ush*. If the *sl-* were to be recognised as a morpheme, we would need to create in our analysis a large set of unique morphs°, which is generally bad practice (see Section 2.2.3). Even in the few cases where we do find some potential for exhaustive analysis, as in *glimmer* and *shimmer*, there is not much gain from the analysis, as we then have to wonder whether there is a *sh-* morph as well.

These phonaesthemes°, then, are morpheme-like in carrying meaning within the word, but not morpheme-like because they do not provide an exhaustive analysis of the word. Their rather vague meaning might also be considered unlike a standard morpheme. They seem to sit somewhere in the penumbra to the morpheme, without fully qualifying as morphemes.

6.6 Blends

Blends° are new words made up by taking the beginning of one word and the end of another; the best blends – in the sense that they are most easily interpreted – have some overlap of phonological material in the middle, as in *guestimate*, from *guess+estimate.* Because there is only one /es/ in *guestimate*, it is impossible to provide a definitive source of the remaining sequence: it could come from *guess* or from *estimate* (though the spelling suggests the latter). It is best not to try to allot the overlapping sequence to individual source words, but just to say that there is some shortening. Other blends may not show such overlap. Some examples are given in (11).

(11) (a) ballute, camcorder, caplet, diesohol (all B), celebutard, tigon
     (b) blaxploitation, boatel, celebutante, computeracy (all B), sexting

The difference between the blends in (11a) and those in (11b) is that those in (11a) denote the mixture or union of the two things in the source words: a *ballute* is a mixture of a balloon and a parachute, a *caplet* is a mixture of a capsule and a tablet, and so on. The forms in (11b), on the other hand, are headed: *computeracy* is a kind of literacy, and the computer is not mixed with the literacy. Some authorities keep the term 'blend' for words like those in (11a), but there is no evidence that the shortening processes are different in the two cases.

It used to be thought that the structure of blends was too unpredictable for any kind of generalisation to be made about their structure. More recent research has shown that this view was overly pessimistic. Although it may not be possible to predict with 100 per cent accuracy what blend will be created from any given pair of words, there is far less flexibility than was once thought, and speakers creating blends are subject to a whole series of phonological and lexical° constraints on what is possible. This is not the place for a full discussion of these constraints. They include things like the following, all of which could carry the proviso that the constraint can be overruled where to maintain it would cause other problems:

- The length of the blend is usually no longer than the length of the longer word in the blend.
- The stress pattern of the blend is usually the same as the stress pattern of the second word in the input to the blend.
- Because the beginnings of words are more easily recognised than the ends of words (see Section 6.3), rather more is usually left of the second input word than of the first.
- More frequent words generally precede less frequent words in the blend.
- If phonological overlap is possible, it is exploited.
- The blend fits with overall patterns of permitted strings of sounds.

- Phonologically similar words are easiest to exploit in blends. *Hangry* is a good blend in formal terms because its input words, *hungry* and *angry*, are so similar.

To summarise, although blends do not necessarily divide words up into classical morphs° (*cam* in *camcorder* is not a morpheme° in *camera*, for instance), there is more regularity in their formation than superficially appears. To the extent that their structure can be shown to be predictable, they are more likely to be seen as having morphological structure: notably, blends work best when their elements are recognisable as words, and thus when their lexical origins are clear. This makes them seem more morphological than if their structure were simply made up of random phoneme sequences from the two source words. At the same time, they are not amenable to analysis in terms of morphemes.

6.7 Clippings

A clipping° is a word shortened from a longer word. Examples include *binocs*, *camo*, *condo*, *deli* (all B), *flu*, *Fro* (B). Most of these have material deleted from the end, but *Fro* (from *Afro*, a hairstyle) has material deleted from the beginning, and *binocs* seems to retain the beginning and the end on the word, while *flu* keeps the middle of *influenza*. While it is probably not coincidence that the majority of these clippings are two syllables long, *flu* and *Fro* show that this is not a necessary outcome, and several of the examples given show that it is not necessarily the stressed syllable which is retained. These examples thus illustrate the lack of predictability of the form of clippings, and the fact that they are forms created by deletion makes them look like the subtractive° forms dealt with in Section 2.2.6, except that the amount of phonological material deleted and its position in the word is not entirely predictable either.

Some clippings are embellished°, usually by the addition of a final *-y* (or *-ie* or *-ey*, all pronounced /i/) or *-o*, as in *aggro*, *boonies*, *ciggie* (all B), *garbo*, *muso*, *possie*, *rellie*. The last four examples here are widespread in Australian English for 'garbage collector', 'musician', 'position' and 'relative/relation'. While embellished clippings are particularly a feature of Australian English, they are also found in English from other parts of the world, as is illustrated by forms such as *baddy*, *bootie*, *Chevvy*, *footy*, *goody*, *homey*, *indie*, *softy*, *tootsie*, *weirdo*. In general terms, the forms here are relatively predictable: the base is made up of as much of the beginning of the word as can fit into a single syllable, and then the embellishment is added (although examples which do not fit this pattern are not particularly hard to find, such as *littlie*, where the syllabic /l/ from *little* is retained). The embellishment is usually treated as a suffix°, but it could simply be phonological supporting material, in which case the *-er(s)* in *Honkers*, *preggers*, *rugger* (British English slang forms from *Hong Kong*, *pregnant* and *rugby*, respectively) and the final vowel in Australian English *Maccas* (from *McDonald's*, the fast food chain) might represent the same phenomenon. It should be noted that many of the clippings cited above like *aggro* and *deli* also end in /i/ or in *-o*, so that drawing the line between embellished clippings and simple clippings can be fraught at times. For instance, although *camo* looks like a simple clipping, the word *camouflage* does not have an /əʊ/ vowel following the /m/, so the final *-o* might be an embellishment.

Sometimes two clippings go together to provide a new lexeme°, as in *capcom* (from *capsule communicator*), *Caricom* (from *Caribbean Community*), *civex* (from *civilian extraction*) (all B), *modem* (from *modulator demodulator*). These are variously referred to as 'clipping compounds', 'complex clippings' and even as 'blends', though there is increasing evidence that they behave differently from blends. It seems that clipping compounds are generally reduced from extant phrases, rather than coined as clipping compounds in the first instance, and their elements are rather less easily reconstituted by listeners for whom the words are unfamiliar than is the case with blends°. Nevertheless, like blends, they are created from the phonological material of words without reference to the morphological structure of those strings, and are not created from sequences of morphs°, in the classical sense. Also, like blends, we can see some of them as headed°, and others as coordinate in structure.

All of these clippings are awkward in traditional morphological terms, partly because of their subtractive° nature, and partly because they are not made up of elements that would form classical morphemes°. They are, however, morphological in the sense that their shape is motivated by forms found elsewhere in the language. Even if their form were totally predictable from the form of the bases, this would be sufficient to put them on the borderline of morphology. Since their form is probably not completely predictable (though again, more than used to be thought), this adds to their marginal status.

6.8 Yiddish-influenced *shm-*

In American English, under the influence of Yiddish, there is a construction where the onset of the first syllable of a word is replaced by the sequence *shm-*. The new form is placed in apposition to the original word, and so does not construct a compound°, or even the same kind of construction° that we saw with rhyme in Section 6.3. Examples are *chemistry, shmemistry*; *eloquent, shmeloquent*; *parked, shmarked*. The meaning is disparaging and dismissive. Just how the construction should be analysed is not clear, but like many of the other examples in this chapter, it is difficult to see *shm-* as a morpheme° in the classical sense, because the rest of the word would become a unique morph°. Note that in this case, /ʃm/ is not an otherwise acceptable onset in English (it also occurs in *shmuck*, another loan from Yiddish), so that English rules concerning the sequencing of phonemes° are not respected.

6.9 Backformation

Backformation° is another type of subtractive° formation. In most instances, something that looks like an affix is deleted to provide a new word. So, for instance, historically *edit* is derived from *editor*, rather than vice versa. *Burglar* (with no *-er* affix) gives rise to the verb *burgle*, which seems to presuppose an analysis of *burglar* as 'one who burgles'. At this level, we might see backformation as a morphological process: a process which undoes morphological structure, even if speakers sometimes make (etymological°) errors of analysis. Other relevant examples are *to axe-murder*, *to cadge*, *to curate*, *to diagnose*, *to proact*, *to surveil(le)* and the nouns *cherry* and *pea* (the original form of the latter was *pease*, reinterpreted as a plural; *cherry* derives from French *cerise*, again reinterpreted as a plural).

However, other examples make clear that this is not what is going on. Examples like *attrit*, *contracept* (both B) and *destruct* indicate that morphology is not being undone. Given *contrition*, parallel to *attrition*, we know that the base is *contrite*, so we would expect *attrite* rather than *attrit*; equally we would expect *contraceive* rather than *contracept*, and the verb corresponding to *destruction* is (normatively) *destroy*. Such examples show that there is deletion here rather than a morphological process based on an appropriate choice of allomorphs. Even so, in these examples, it is a morph which is deleted, and that seems to be at least a marginally morphological process.

But there are other forms like *jacuze* ('what one does in a Jacuzzi'), where there is no deletion of a morph. This looks rather more like clipping°. It is not necessarily unmotivated clipping, though. *Abuse*, *accuse*, *amuse*, *bemuse*, *diffuse*, *enthuse*, *excuse*, *infuse*, *refuse*, which rhyme with *jacuze*, are all verbs, and there do not appear to be any disyllabic non-verbs that rhyme. So *jacuze* fits into a paradigm° of verbs which motivate it.

Backformation is a process which looks as though it is tied to morphemes in some instances, but which is not always tied to things which can be described as morphemes. In some instances, like *jacuze*, the motivation for the word seems to be much wider than the kind of pattern that morphology usually pays attention to.

6.10 Messy formations and the limits of description

Barnhart et al. (1990) provide etymologies for a number of words which do not seem to fit into any of these types at all, or at least not easily. Some examples are provided in (12), with the etymology° as provided by Barnhart et al.

(12)	*word*	*source*
	amoxycillin	AMino-hydrOXYphenyl + peniCILLIN
	ASAT	AntiSATellite interceptor
	aspartame	ASPARTic acid + phenylAlamine Methyl Ester
	benzodiazepine	benzo (< benzine) + di- + -az (nitrogen) + -epi +-ine
	CTOL	Conventional Take-Off and Landing
	cumecs	CUbic MEtres per Second (2nd <c> apparently unaccounted for)

The words in (12) are all technical words, and have been created with care. In some ways this seems different from the unconscious productivity° of inflectional morphology, or even the use of derivational affixes illustrated in (16)–(22) below. Some authorities (e.g. Schultink 1961) have suggested that consciously created words are not part of morphology, because they do not represent the productivity inherent in the system, but the effects of analysis on existing words. The difficulty with such a viewpoint is that it does not seem to be a principle which can be applied in real cases. Was the first use of *ciggie* created by someone who was conscious of what they were doing, or automatically produced by the rules of English, and what noticeable difference would there be that could provide a clue for the linguist as analyst that it was one or the other? The answer may well be that there is no difference in kind between consciously and subconsciously formed words, but that the rarer the models and the more knowledge that is required to perceive the structure in the models, the more difficult it is to create new words according to those models, and so the more conscious the formation process will appear.

Whatever the status of words like those in (12), they raise questions as to the limits of morphology: what counts as motivation in these forms seems rather different from what counts as motivation in the formation of *comes* or *Moroccanisation* (B). But in both cases the form of words is being created in a non-random manner on the basis of some semantic demand.

A final question which needs to be considered is the extent to which the types of formation that have been discussed in this chapter are independent types. The alternative is that they are all variants on a single type, or in a penumbra around one or more than one canonical° type. In some senses, it does not matter: the speakers who coin the words are not interested in the scientific classification of the words that are created. From a taxonomic point of view, though, the fuzzy borders between types might make better sense if these are not all independent of each other, and if the variability that is found in practice is due in part to the amount of conscious deliberation that lies behind the word-creation.

6.11 Analogy

At some point, words are created whose model may be clear but where there is no morphology and no regular pattern involved. Some examples are given below.

(13) You wouldn't get stars staying there, only wannabes and usetabes. (Barry Norman, *Death on Sunset*, London: Orion, 1998, p. 93)
(14) Plenty of electronic gadgetry and expensive crappolata. (John Francome, *Rough Ride*, London: Headline, 1992, p. 128)
(15) If magic was in the ear of the behearer . . . then Lucy seemed ready to settle for that. (Gavin Lyall, *Spy's Honour*, London: Hodder & Stoughton, 1993, p. 310)

In such cases we would probably cease talking about word-formation or morphology and talk about analogy. Cases of analogy might create a pattern, but are not part of an existing pattern, and there is only one model available to allow them to be formed. It might not even be clear what the model is (as with (14) above).

However, if the acceptance of analogy is a useful strategy for the linguist, then it is not clear where the boundaries of analogy should go. Consider, for instance, the following examples.

(16) Like the world is divided into stomp*ers* and stomp*ees* and he's a stomp*ee*. (Stephen Dobyns, *Saratoga Strongbox*, New York: Viking, 1998, p. 46; italics in the original)
(17) What it needed was to match solicitor with solicitee. (Michael Thomas, *Hard Money*, New York: Viking, 1983, p. 191)

(18) The bellower was Harmon Crundall – and the bellowee the mysterious Mrs Smith. (Joan Hess, *Murder at the Murder at the Mimosa Inn*, New York: St. Martin's Press, 1986, p. 41)
(19) The stab*ber* might want to stay friends but not the stab*bee.* (Richard Laymon, *Night in the Lonesome October*, London: Headline, 2001, p. 29; italics in the original)
(20) I found myself more therapist with Julie than therapee. (Robert B. Parker, *Perish Twice*, London: Murray, 2000, p. 26)
(21) He womanises, I man-ise. (Susan Moody, *The Italian Garden*, London: Hodder & Stoughton, 1994, p. 69)
(22) An open-plan living-room with 'kitchenette' downstairs and a bedroomette and bathroomette upstairs. (David Lodge, *Thinks*, London: Secker & Warburg, 2001, p. 10)

Should all of these examples also be cases of analogy, since the source of the analogy is clearly given in the citations? While most linguists have resisted this line, Becker (1990) argues that rules are really just analogies, but repeated analogies. In a similar vein, the question is posed in Bauer (2012) as to whether there is any real difference between a blend such as *celebutard* (presumably from *celebrity* + *retard*) and, say, *bedroomette*, from *bedroom* + *kitchenette.* The question is not answered in that paper, but it is not clear how the speaker constructs these forms or how the linguist should best analyse them.

What we can see is that the form of words can be determined or motivated by a number of different facets of other words, and that not all these impulses are necessarily morphological in the standard sense of requiring morphemes. What we might say is that varying impulses come together in the creation of new words, and when the result of the creation is such that we have consistent form being related to consistent meaning, then we talk about morphology. The morphological part of word-formation, though, is just that – a part, not all that there is to word-formation.

Notes and comments

The expression *slip, slap, slop* in (7) is the slogan of the campaign in New Zealand to prevent skin cancer: when in the sun one should slip on a shirt, slap on a hat and slop on sunscreen. It is of particular interest in that it contains both /ɪ/-/æ/ apophony and /ɪ/-/ɒ/ apophony, the two major patterns of apophony° in such constructions.

In this chapter, the example words not listed in Barnhart et al. (1990) are attested, but are not necessarily as recent (though many words in

Barnhart et al. 1990 are now over fifty years old). Barnhart et al. provide not only datings but also citations and, usefully for the discussion in this chapter, the linguistic sources of the words.

At least two papers have independently proposed that the categories discussed in this chapter (or some subset of them) are not independent, but illustrate variability within some larger categories. They are Bauer (1998a) and López Rúa (2002), and the views they present are very different. It is not clear to me whether there is any advantage to trying to further such an analysis, but some explanation is required for why the categories are not always easily distinguishable.

One category that has been omitted here – mainly because it raises so many questions – is the category of neoclassical compounds. These are words like *geology*, *photograph*, *suicide*, *television* which are made up of elements from the classical languages Latin and Greek, even when the compounds themselves are not words from that era. For some discussion of these, see Bauer (2017b).

Reading

My view of blends° has been very strongly influenced by the work of my student Natalia Beliaeva. See also the work of Lappe (2007) and the state-of-the-art presentations in Renner et al. (2012). Lappe (2007) is also a good source on clippings°, and Beliaeva (2014) has again influenced my view of clipping compounds.

On Yiddish-influenced *shm-*, see Bauer et al. (2013: 413), from where the examples are taken.

On phonaesthemes°, see Bergen (2004) and Kwon and Round (2015). The label comes from Firth ([1930] 1964).

Discussion questions

Some suggested answers to these questions can be found in the Answers to Discussion Questions at edinburghuniversitypress.com/rethinkingmorphology

1. Many brand names are made up from scratch (and not reused names, like *Citroën*, or ordinary words, like *Jaguar*). Celebrated examples are *Exxon* and *Kodak*. Collect as many such words as you can. Do they contain any morphology, in the classical sense? Do they make use of such phonological patterns as rhyme, assonance, alliteration, and so on? Do they exploit phonaesthemes? Are their

meanings (in the sense of the nature of the product they name) at all derivable from their forms?

2. Some abbreviations seem to have a form which could be either an acronym° or an initialism°. The form *faq* was cited in the chapter, *JAL* is another. How many such forms can you find? Are there any principles determining which way they are pronounced?
3. Consider the words in (12), or look in any dictionary of neologisms to find further examples. To what extent can these words be seen as complying with the demands of classical morpheme-based analysis? Is there a morpheme {e} in *email*? Are these words different in principle from acronyms°? Explain your answer.

7 Exemplars and resonances

7.1 Interlude: the acquisition of phonemes

As linguists, we are taught the importance of phonemes° in allowing for the expression of contrasting words: we test for phonemes by using minimal pairs° (so that the pair *sopping* and *sobbing*, with contrasting meanings, establishes that /p/ contrasts with /b/ in English), but there is an important sense in which the relationship is the other way round – the fact that phonemes contrast in this way makes it possible to express different meanings. By the time we learn linguistics, the notion of the phoneme seems fairly self-explanatory, especially if we have been raised speaking a language which uses an alphabet for its writing system, even if the theoretical details of phonemic analysis may be confusing. That is because we have already come across the notion that different letters represent the different sounds that we perceive as important. By the time we have learnt to read we have also learnt to ignore as trivial all kinds of allophonic information. Speakers who routinely have different phonetic qualities for the two /l/s in *lull*, for instance, may be surprised to discover this when they start studying phonetics.

But children in the beginning stages of learning their mother tongue do not have any of this information about phonemes. The data from which they learn their language contains all the minute phonetic detail, but the phonemes are not given in the data. Phonemes must emerge from the child's analysis of the input, the input itself does not supply them. Although children may know individual words which can be used to form minimal pairs, like *cat*, *hat*, *sat*, *that* in English, they are not presented in contrasting sets. Furthermore, children very probably do not know enough words to establish the complete phonemic inventory of the language they are learning. It is only when they are taught rhymes or come to read (or be read) works which feature minimal pairs (like *The Cat in the Hat* (Seuss 1957) for English) that they are presented with minimal pairs in contrasting environments. Moreover, they do not necessarily know what in the phonetic input is important, and what is speaker- or context-dependent. Kelly and Local (1989: 40) give transcriptions from a five-year-old child undergoing speech therapy who knows the words *hat* and *bag*, but ends them both with a glottal stop. However, this does not mean that they are identical to *hag* and *bat*. The difference between the word-final voiceless° plosive and the word-final voiced° plosive is maintained by two things: the length of the vowel, which is longer in *bag* than in *hat*, and the fact that the glottal stop is released in *hat* ([$ʔ^h$]) and not in *bag* (and this generalises to other words as well). The child is reproducing valuable pieces of the phonetic input, but has not yet learned to make the difference between a final [t] and a final [g] in a way that an adult speaker can recognise. Thus the child's production pays attention to phonetic detail that adults do not perceive before the child is able to produce sounds which will function as phonemes for the listener.

In order to do this, children must be aware of a large amount of phonetic detail and have done a great deal of analysis of the speech that they are hearing. The child transcribed by Kelly and Local is not yet producing things which an adult can process in terms of adult phonemes: the phonetic form precedes the emergence of the phonemic structure.

7.2 Acquiring morphology

The acquisition of morphology must take place in the same way. The child is not presented with morphemes or morphs, but with words and phrases. The child's first job is to isolate the words, and once that is done, recurrent pieces of form within the words can be scanned to see whether they match with meaning in any useful way. Since it is entirely possible to use a morphologically complex form in a completely coherent way without knowing that it is morphologically complex, we need more evidence than the use of such forms to indicate that morphological structure is being processed. Even adult speakers frequently do not realise that *dearth* is related to *dear*, that *filth* is related to *foul* and that *month* is related to *moon* (though it must be admitted that it is not necessarily clear that the relationship here is morphological rather than just etymological°). One experimental task found that adult speakers did not relate *citizenship* to *citizen* (Wheeler and Schumsky 1980).

The first evidence of children using morphology is when they make mistakes with it. Children who have appropriately used words like *came* and *went* for some time will suddenly start using the forms *comed* and *goed*, which have never formed part of their input (and so, which they have not learned as ready-made items). Such forms indicate that they have analysed the make-up of regular past tense forms and acquired the ability to generalise the marking of the past tense. They soon manage to sort out the irregular verbs from the regular ones, and the system settles down to resemble the adult system.

The place where children are most likely to make the first use of morphology is in inflection°. This is because the inflectional affixes are the most common affixes, the ones that are heard most often. For the child to make a good analysis, particularly in the early stages, input containing both repeated affixes° and repeated bases° is required. The repeated bases are guaranteed by the relatively limited vocabulary used to pre-lingual children, and the repeated affixes are guaranteed by the frequency of inflection. In a language like English, bases in isolation are also guaranteed because base-forms of verbs occur in the imperative, in the infinitive (which is also used in the future: *will see*, *are going to see*) and in the non-third-person singular, and the base-form of nouns occurs in the singular. More heavily inflecting languages do not provide as many forms with bare stems°, but the stem is repeated across a number of inflected forms (or if there are multiple stems, they too are repeated in different inflected forms). If the relevant language has bare stems at all, the form of the verb most likely to show no marking (to have a bare stem) in verbs is either the imperative, or the first person singular, or the third person singular – all used fairly frequently, even to children (see Mayerthaler 1981).

Where words are rarer and the processes less generalised°, the learning of morphology takes longer. The pair *vain/vanity*, for instance, is likely to be learned much later than the inflected forms of irregular verbs, simply because of relative frequency. Other factors such as the relative learnedness of Latin-based morphology in English are part of what causes this difference in frequency. But the pattern is also very much less predictable. *Sane/sanity* matches *vain/vanity* in phonological (if not orthographic°) terms, but there is no **planity* to correspond to *plain*. Also, although we find *deprave/depravity* with a similar phonological alternation, *deprave* is a verb, not an adjective, so that the parallel is not as close as it might be. Accordingly, there is evidence that some speakers (perhaps all speakers) never get to the point of being able to use such alternations to create new words themselves (Bauer 1983: 138 and sources there), though they may recognise them in some pairs of words.

7.3 Exemplar theory

Exemplar theory is originally a psychological theory about how humans perceive and classify the world. We learn a concept like 'bird', the theory goes, by meeting individual exemplars of birds, and eventually end up with a category of bird which excludes fairies, mosquitoes and pterosaurs, includes sparrows, macaws, ostriches and penguins, and allows aeroplanes only as metaphors. Because we see more sparrows than we see ostriches, and because most of the exemplars we see have shorter necks than ostriches and are closer in size to sparrows than to ostriches, some birds are more central to our notion of what a bird is than others are.

Where language is concerned, the idea is that we meet various exemplars of individual categories, each of which we remember. For the purposes of this exposition, let us assume that the category we meet is the word, though we clearly meet categories both larger and smaller than the word as well. When we hear a given word, we add the memory of that word to our cloud of memories of that word. Not only do we remember particular phonetic detail, but we remember social and linguistic information that goes with the word, perhaps 'female speaker', 'young speaker', 'spoken in jest', and what the adjacent words were (Foulkes 2010). The more tokens of the word we hear, the more accurate our picture of the word in our speech community becomes, but that does not necessarily mean that it becomes more precise: as we hear more tokens, we also hear more variability and build that into our picture of the word concerned. As we learn words, we also learn about the sounds which make up those words. Because we learn from the exemplars and not from some pre-defined phonetic system, we learn the precise phonetic detail of the sounds which are used in our speech community: thus /p/ is not phonetically identical in Dutch, English, French and Thai, but speakers learn about one of these and learn the phonetic detail of the language (or languages) they are surrounded by. As the cloud of exemplars increases, it allows us to predict which category any given phonetic input belongs to, and provides us with a target to aim for in our own output. Because our own output may not be entirely accurate (indeed, it is not, since surrounding material draws us away from an 'ideal' pronunciation), our outputs add to the cloud of exemplars heard by other speakers, and so on.

Just how much is stored over what time period and how fast these memories decay is not clear. It is clear that our perceptions of a category can be influenced by recent experience (Cutler 2010; Chua 2016), so that not only frequency of the input but also recency of the input are relevant factors in our perception of the categories we perceive (and so, presumably, attempt to reproduce).

How does this apply to morphology? Again we hear and store words in our memories. With those words we also store information such as 'scientific', 'disparaging', 'baby talk' and the meanings of the words as far as we are able to deduce them, including such things as 'plural' and 'past'. As we hear clusters of words, so we also hear clusters of parts of words, and those clusters we hear most frequently will be most strongly associated with each other. Frequency is vital here: we do not construct *bes* as the third person singular of BE, despite the high frequency of *-s* which marks this category, because the frequency of *is* in the appropriate context is even greater.

When we need a morphologically complex word, we have two ways in which to find it. Either we can look in our memories to see whether a suitable word is already available, or we can try to construct one. Any model which allows the two possibilities simultaneously is called a 'dual route°' model, as opposed to models which presume that only one of these options is available. Where the morphologically complex word is more common than its base, we will generally arrive at that word first (Hay 2003); when the base is more common than the derived word, we may take either route. So we probably do not invent *government* every time we need it (we find it in our memories), but we might have to invent *indecipherability*. When we need to invent a word, we search in our set of stored words for suitable analogies from which to create a new word. Where classical morphemes are available, they will make good patterns, providing they are frequent enough or recent enough in our memory, but other patterns are also available, as we have seen in Chapter 6 and as we shall see immediately below. What we take as the best, or most available, pattern may not be the same for every individual, so that there is always the possibility that speakers will produce different forms to fit the same requirements. On the other hand, some analogies are so frequent in our experience that they are likely to be called upon whenever needed (and this might be the case with the obvious inflections).

Consider a concrete example. You may not know an adjective corresponding to the noun *forest* (though larger dictionaries do list such adjectives, so your experience may provide you with a memorised word). In English, we can often escape such problems by using the noun, so that we might talk of *forest trees*, *forest creatures* and the like. We might think of a (near) synonym° for *forest*, like *woods*, *bush*, *jungle*, and create an adjective from one of those, if appropriate. *Woodsy* and *bushy* both have wrong meanings. So we look for parallels with other affixes: *-ish*, *-ful*, *-able*, *-some*, *-y* and *-esque* all have specific and inappropriate meanings, *-ic* prefers classical bases, *-ous* is not used much on new forms, but *-al*/*-ar*, *-(i)an*, *-ary*/*-ory* all seem potentially available, and then it is a matter of what the best form is on the basis of other factors: rhyming words, words with the same stress pattern, and so on.

The best parallels would be the ones which are most familiar, because most frequent or most recently met (which in many cases will be the same thing). *Vestal* is a possible influence; there is no parallel ending in *-estan*, or *-estary*/*-estory*. *Forestal* is listed by some dictionaries. You may be able to think of alternatives.

There is no implication that such a process would be conscious, or as drawn-out as I have made it sound. It would be automatic on the basis of the patterns available in memory.

The difference between the dual-route° model described above and other versions of a dual-route model is that there is no default form here, no rule to fall back on which gives an answer in cases of uncertainty. The answer has to arise from the unconscious analysis of patterns in memory. This means that not all speakers will necessarily come to the same conclusion (some dictionaries list *forestine* as a possible adjective from *forest*). In the final analysis, if a speaker needs a word to fill a gap, even a word which cannot be fully justified on the basis of available patterns will be better than no word at all.

Just what makes a suitable pattern is a matter of some interest. It has already been implied that more things than just morphemes in the classical sense may be involved (see Chapter 6). Hockett (1987) considers such matters in detail.

7.4 Resonances

Hockett (1987) provides a critique of structuralist morphology, which he calls 'morphemics'. He complains about what he calls (1987: 82) 'the great agglutinative° fraud' in the way that the word-based morphologists do. He also complains that there are all kinds of structures which cannot be represented within morphemics – and we have discussed many of these in Chapter 6. But Hockett goes beyond things which might be considered marginal morphology into things which would definitely not be considered morphology.

Hockett points out that puns cause associations between words which are non-morphological. We can cite examples from Shakespeare such as

> Thus is the will of a living daughter
> Curb'd by the will of a dead father

when Portia's father's last will and testament prevents her from doing what she wants to do. Or (spoken by a cobbler)

> I meddle not with men's matters, nor with women's matters but with awl.

Hockett also points out that some words have allusions attached to them, either short-term allusions or more established ones. Short-term allusions may operate within a text, as in the following extracts from a novel.

> (p. 51) I saw a woman standing in the lighted kitchen, leaning back against a counter. In her left hand was a bottle of tequila [. . .] (p. 152) The tequila woman almost certainly lived in the house. (Richard Laymon, *Night in the Lonesome October*, London: Headline, 2001)

Longer-term allusions may be of many kinds, and may be institutionalised or personal. Consider, first, the following literary example.

> 'Connected' is a dangerous word in tabloidese, saturated with carnal implications. (Bryan Forbes, *The Twisted Playground*, London: Heinemann, 1993, p. 10)

Another literary allusion is in Sir Ernest Gowers's use of the blend *Barnacular* (from *Barnacle* + *vernacular*), with reference to the Barnacle family, who run the circumlocution office in Dickens's *Little Dorrit*. References to something being rotten in the state of Denmark go back to Shakespeare's *Hamlet*. Huge numbers of expressions in English can be linked back to the Bible, to Shakespeare, to the *Book of Common Prayer*, and the like. Consider *physician, heal thyself*, *star-crossed lovers*, *for better or for worse*. The phrase *more than somewhat* originated with Damon Runyon, but became serious when its link with the author was lost (see Partridge 1985).

Hockett (1987: 72) points out that even Malapropisms (another literary reference!) can link words. I heard of someone recently who believed that the phrase was *rope learning* instead of *rote learning*. *Rope* gains new associations from the phrase. If you think there is a word *upmost* but no word *utmost* (as in *to do one's utmost*), then *up* has meanings for you that it does not necessarily have for other speakers. The common formulation of *chaise lounge* for *chaise longue* suggests actions appropriate for the piece of furniture. The original Mrs Malaprop talks about *the contagious countries* instead of *the contiguous countries*. On the news the day I wrote this section I heard of a policeman who was *recommended* for his behaviour, when presumably he was actually *commended*. The link between *commend* and *recommend* is revitalised. A spelling (in an American source) of *make due* rather than *make do* suggests new links for that idiom (David Ellis, *Line of Vision*, New York: Putnam, 2001, p. 61), as does the sentence *[H]e bordered trolleybus No 5 [. . .] to the town centre* in an Australian book (Sandy McCutcheon, *Delicate Indecencies*, Sydney: HarperCollins, 2001, p. 89).

Folk etymology° is another category that Hockett mentions. 'Folk etymology' is a rather outdated term for another kind of morphological reanalysis, one that is not historically justified. *Female*, for instance, is borrowed from French *femelle*, which is not formally linked to *male*; a *woodchuck* has nothing to do with either *wood* or throwing, but is a reinterpretation of a foreign word; *mushrooms* have nothing, etymologically° or logically, to do with *room*. Nevertheless, connections can be drawn between the borrowed word and its falsely assumed origin because of their form. These are, from an academic point of view, false etymologies, but that does not mean that they are not real to speakers, just as real as genuine etymologies. Real etymologies, too, can cause links between words, as we say in Section 2.2.2 with words like *deceive*, *perceive*, *receive*.

As Hockett (1987: 73–4) points out, we may not necessarily have a single set of associations with a word. Given frankfurter sausages from Frankfurt and limburger cheese from Limburg, we can see a hamburger patty as coming from Hamburg. But we also have another set of parallels, with *beef burger*, *cheese burger*, *chicken burger*, *fish burger* and the like, which leads us to think of a hamburger as a burger somehow related to ham (even though ham is perhaps one of the few meats that does not appear to be used in them!). There is no reason to suppose that we can see only one of these patterns: both can operate simultaneously.

Hockett terms all these links, and indeed any others that you can think of, 'resonances°'. Resonances may be phonological, formal, idiomatic, semantic, pragmatic; they may be general to a community of speakers or entirely personal; there may be one or several supporting any particular word. Hockett states explicitly, in a way that is completely in conflict with the approach taken by Saussure or by Chomsky,

> It does not matter that the line of association is personal, since all such associations are personal, and all that varies is their strength and how widely they are shared. (Hockett 1987: 76)

In 1987, the approach taken by Hockett here was not compatible with any linguistic theory, and as a result his views were, rather unfortunately, I think, largely ignored. But resonances are entirely compatible with exemplar theory. Hockett (1987: 89) specifically links resonances to first language acquisition, saying that the child can use resonances as a motivation for the analysis of new words (and for the creation of new forms). Anyone with children will have stories of children who got the patterns 'wrong' (by adult standards) and came up with a form which, however well justified, was not an institutionalised form in the speech community. Some of these forms become institutionalised within the family, but rarely go beyond those limits. Some do. Many students in the University department within which I worked seemed to think that if *precede* meant 'to come before', *proceed* must mean 'to come after', and used it that way in essays. Thus are new usages created.

If we accept Hockett's resonances as factors affecting the way in which words are perceived, analysed and created, then classical morphology, Hockett's 'morphemics', is simply a special kind of resonance. Where the resonances happen to have form and meaning in agreement, and where the resonances happen to analyse a word with nothing left over, we have classical morphology. There may, indeed, be a special place for such resonances; but they are not the only forces operating in understanding and producing words.

7.5 Why is an approach based on exemplar theory and resonances an improvement?

In this section, we return to some of the issues that have previously been raised, and where we have found theoretical problems, and look at them again within the framework of exemplar theory and Hockett's resonances. Not all of the issues that are raised by morpheme-based morphology need to be revisited. Many of the constructions considered in Chapter 6 look rather different in the light of exemplar theory and resonances than they do in a framework which includes morphemes, but there is little to be gained by revisiting them in turn. On the other hand, there are some issues which the new theoretical approach raises, where we can contrast the new with some or all of the models that have already been considered. The overall conclusion will be that exemplar theory and the theory of resonances allow us to include rather more in a theory of word structure with rather fewer theoretical problems. It is to be hoped that this is achieved without impoverishing the theoretical relevance and unity of dealing with a theory of word structure.

7.5.1 Morphemes

Once we start looking for resonances° rather than for morphemes°, we no longer have to worry about whether a word is exhaustively analysed into a sequence of meaningful elements or whether there is a unique analysis of that word. Any resonance or set of resonances can provide valuable material for generalisations on the part of a speaker. It will probably still be the case that the most productive° resonances will be the ones which we have previously thought of as being morphemic, because of the factors, such as exhaustivity and form-meaning links, which make us set up morphemes in the first place. But we do not have to reject outright, for example, phonaesthemes°, as being legitimate grounds for association in the creation of new forms.

The theoretical advantage is then that we do not have to worry about all the problems that there are with morphemes. If morphemes are not our fundamental unit of analysis, then the fact that there are theoretical problems with morphemes is irrelevant. The problem with morphemes has never been that they lack psychological validity or that we cannot build up new words using them, the problem has been that there are some places where they do not seem to work as expected. If we are looking for the cognitively real building blocks, many morphemes will still be in our list, but they operate alongside other cognitively real structures. Using exemplar theory and resonances simply means that the entire burden of form–meaning relationships is not placed on a single type of unit.

Will new problems arise because some resonances do not appear to be exploited? To use a well-known example, is it a problem that the word *ear* is related semantically to the word *hear*, yet that similarity does not seem to be exploited in the formation of new words? Or is it a problem that *car*, *cockle*, *commencement* and *curve* all begin with a <c>? There may well be personal resonances in some of these instances, but it seems unlikely that they are frequent enough or salient enough to give rise to new words on their basis. If they did, by any chance, it is not clear that other speakers would recognise them (with the corollary that they might not adopt the new word).

7.5.2 Unique outcomes

One potential problem that has not previously been raised, because it has not been relevant until now, is the way recent models of linguistics have functioned. Most generative theories of language, which have dominated linguistics for over fifty years, predict the outcomes of the processes they employ by way of rules. Rules are statements of observed regularity. The general pattern is that, given a particular input, the output is totally predicted by the rules. Earlier models of linguistics were more concerned with analysing linguistic patterns than predicting outputs, and so this focus on outputs did not arise in the early days of morpheme-based morphology. Typically (though not necessarily universally), rule-based approaches tend to predict a unique outcome for a given question. 'What is the plural of *mouse*?' sounds like a relevant question for a morphologist or grammarian, when 'What are the possible plurals of *mouse*?' might be a better one. As it happens, English speakers cumulatively have at least three possible plurals of *mouse* – *mice*, *mouses* and (for those that recall the cartoon mice Pixie and Dixie, and the two mice's nemesis Mr Jinks) *meeces* – used largely in the phrase *I hate those meeces to pieces*. While alternative outcomes for morphological structures may not be overwhelmingly common in the inflectional morphology of many languages, they are reported from several languages, and the fact that they occur at all is significant (see, e.g., Thornton 2012; Bauer 2013/14). Exemplar theory specifically allows for multiple outcomes, depending on things like style, speaker identity, context, and so on.

7.5.3 Inflection and derivation

The distinction between inflection and derivation may still be compatible with the view of morphology espoused here, but it is not necessary. The distinction can be largely one of frequency (and in many cases, regularity), which means that the patterns in inflection are more familiar than those in derivation (see Hay 2003: 18). If the patterns are more regular and more frequent, they are easier to use as models for new formations. This ease of application is enhanced by the number of times the speaker has to apply the models to create new forms.

However, if the fundamental issue here is not whether a particular piece of morphology or formal structure is inflectional or derivational, but rather how frequent it is and, deriving from that and other factors, how easily it is applied in previously unfamiliar cases, it is totally irrelevant whether we can provide a definition of inflection and derivation which creates two neat sub-types of structure or not. Inflection and derivation may not even be relevant categories, but rather a proxy for highly frequent and predictable versus less frequent and less predictable. If that is the case, we need not ask whether something is inflectional or derivational, but how recognisable it is as a chunk which can be used in new analogies. If it is then the case, as claimed by Hay (2003: 17), that the most recognisable affixes are external to (further from the root° than) less easily recognised ones (Hay does not use those terms), then even the ordering of inflectional and derivational affixes is not a result of their categorial status as inflectional or derivational, but a result of other factors such as frequency and regularity.

7.5.4 Morphotactics

Morphotactics° is less problematic under this kind of approach than it is under a strict word-syntax approach. If new words are created by analogies with old words, the same sequences of morphs are likely to recur. New sequences of morphs occur when new affixes are added to words with old sequences of morphs in them. For this to be the case, the new morphs° added have to be easily recognisable and very productive°. In general terms, they also have to be more general° in their application and less likely to cause important semantic change to the word to which they are added. In fact, semantically, we would expect them to treat the material to which they are added as a unit – which would give rise to the general pattern of affixes having scope° over material closer to the root° than themselves. In other words, the kinds of patterns that we see when we look at morphotactics, and which might there appear to be problematic in terms of theoretical interpretation, seem to follow fairly automatically from a notion that the most productive pieces of word structure are likely to be affixal, and that the patterns affecting such affixes are likely to be determined by previously experienced patterns.

The same process explains many so-called 'ordering paradoxes°'. A form such as *transformational grammarian* does not denote a grammarian who is transformational, but a person who deals with transformational grammar. The semantic bracketing needs to be [*transformational grammar*]*ian*, but that seems to confuse the levels of syntax and morphology: the morphology applies to a syntactic structure as its base. But if we consider that there are two analogies here, an analogy with *transformational grammar* and an analogy with *grammarian*, there is no real paradox, since both are in the experience of the speaker at the time at which *transformational grammarian* is coined. The same is true with paradoxes such as *unhappier*. The comparative° *-er* is not generally added to trisyllabic adjectives (Alice in Wonderland's *curiouser and curiouser* is a joke which has become part of English, but *defensiver* sounds odd). So it is odd to find it added to trisyllabic *unhappy*. But speakers have familiarity with *unhappy* and familiarity with *happier*, so *unhappier* is explicable, even if it is not necessarily what would be predicted. We can see this as resonances from existing words or the influence of memorised exemplars on the new formation. We do not need to see any paradox at all.

7.5.5 Headedness

There is theoretical discussion, even today, as to whether compounds° are best treated as morphological structures, syntactic structures, or some mixture of both. It is certainly true that compounds are the most syntax-like type of word-formation°, and there is a certain amount of evidence that, at least in some languages, some compounds are derived from syntactic structures. For example, the linking elements in German compounds such as *Maschine-n-bau* 'machine-LINK-build = mechanical engineering' can mostly be traced back to inflectional affixes° which may, at one time, have allowed nouns to co-occur in a syntactic construction°. Whatever the proper analysis of these linking elements (see Neef 2015), they no longer have that function and are, in some way, lexical°. They do, though, illustrate the close relationship between syntax° and compounding.

That being the case, it is perhaps not particularly surprising that headedness°, a notion developed within syntax, applies relatively well to compounds, and less well to other kinds of morphological construction. Nor is it surprising that the order of head and modifier in syntax should so often be reflected in the order of head and modifier in compounds (Bauer 2001), even though there is no complete match. Once speakers try to generalise over structures that are right-headed, they construct more right-headed structures.

Where the parallel to syntax is less overt, as in derivation°, the value of headedness becomes less obvious. Although there a few suffixes of English which we know to have their origins in potentially free° words (affixes like *-dom*, *-hood* and *-ly*), the transition to affixhood implies losing some syntactic qualities, perhaps including the ability to show headedness in the syntactic sense. Suffixes, though, at least in English, have the quality of being able to determine word-class in words. This might be somethings which arises historically as a remnant of their former position as heads, or it may be a completely separate phenomenon. There is one place, however, where this general pattern is broken in English. Negative/reversative/privative verbs derived from nouns (*behead*, *defrock*, *disrobe*, *unhorse*) have their word-class determined by the prefix. When we look at the possible parallels, we might be able to see why. Although there are many ways of making negatives in English, the default, for many centuries, seems to have been *un-*. It is used fundamentally on adjectives (*unavoidable*, *unhappy*, *unrighteous*), but is also found on verbal bases (*unban*, *unbend*, *unfasten*, *unhitch*), and even more, on bases that are past participles (*unalloyed*, *unborn*, *unfenced*), and which can be read as presupposing the relevant verbs (?*unalloy*, ?*unbear*, ?*unfence*). We seem to have a pattern where there are potential verbs whose superficial structure contains a prefix and a noun. There are also verbs like *uncover*, *uncurl* which we could read as being derived from verbs *cover* and *curl*, and as being right-headed. However, *cover* and *curl* are also nouns, so verbs like this may look as though they are left-headed, creating verbs from nouns. We have one other way of making such verbs in English, and that is by conversion°: *to dust* means 'to remove dust from ~', *to weed* means 'to remove weeds from ~', and so on. This pattern is used to denote addition as well as removal: *to paint* means 'to add paint to ~', *to salt* means 'to add salt to ~', and so on. Some words, like *dust*, have both meanings: *to dust the furniture* is to remove dust, while *to dust the cake* *with icing sugar* is to add (something that looks like) dust. In principle, *to robe* might mean 'to remove a robe from ~', but it also means 'to dress someone in a robe', and so adding a negative marker makes it clear which is intended. All the parallels, whether genuine or reanalysed, suggest that to create a negative verb from a noun you should add a negative prefix, and that that negative prefix will be class-changing. By copying the patterns already in the language, you strengthen one of the few instances of left-headedness in English, and you copy it because there is no alternative pattern to copy.

The general conclusion here is that what is viewed as headedness in derivational morphology may arise from a generalisation of existing patterns of derivation°, rather than from the imposition of a particular pattern of headedness of derivatives°.

7.5.6 Lack of compositionality

We have already seen (Section 7.2) that speakers may use morphologically complex words without being aware of their internal make-up. You do not have to be able to link *cockerel* to *mackerel* to use *cockerel* perfectly appropriately. So we can see that the meanings of words, even words which are morphologically complex, can, to some extent, be independent of their morphological make-up.

This is more often seen as being problematic when the meaning of a morphologically complex word can be seen as containing elements that cannot be linked to any element of form. Consider the word *textbook*. It may not be absolutely clear how we are to interpret *textbook*: is it a book that contains texts, or is it a book that is used as a text? In either case, the form *textbook* does not say anything about a textbook being 'used especially in schools and colleges' (Hornby 2000), about whether it is published or presented as a loose-leaf folder with photocopied pages, about the size of a textbook, about expectations for layout and the use of diagrams or pictures in a textbook (matters which are generalisations, and not necessarily true of every single textbook), and so on. This means that speakers have a lot of information about a textbook which is not reflected in the form *textbook*.

Consider a reconstituted history of the word. The original user of the term may not have had a specific meaning in mind, but wanted to relate the book to texts in some way, and felt that what distinguished this book from others was its relationship with text or with texts. *Textbook* thus became a label for the object, and was used by generations of students. The students did not need to know how to interpret the relationship between *text* and *book* in order to use it. They were exposed to the word *textbook* in many exemplars, and with each exposure had a physical object to relate that exemplar to. Their interpretation of *textbook* thus became the sum of their exemplars, a cloud of experiences all of which are suitably termed 'textbooks', although they differ in various respects, and some of the features will be more frequent than others (given developments in publishing, these features may not be the same for speakers of different generations). Inevitably, speakers have more information about textbooks than is formally coded in the label *textbook*. No useful word could formally mark all the things we know about textbooks (even if we could find an agreed core of accepted features). There is, though, a real question as to which parts of the meaning are 'linguistic' and which parts are 'encyclopedic', and whether it matters, or whether it is even the case that the two can in principle be distinguished.

Similar problems arise with derivation. We can, for instance, distinguish several meanings of *sleeper*: 'person who sleeps or is asleep', 'train in which one can sleep', 'coach of a train in which one can sleep', 'beam on which railway tracks are laid' (in American English called a *tie*), 'product that shows sudden success some time after being launched', 'object placed in pierced ears while sleeping', and others. Each has (or had at coining) a relationship with *sleep* which motivated the formation. Each is learnt individually by users of English, and has its own cloud of usages, and fits into a pattern of other formations, as illustrated in (1), where words with a similar pattern of formation are listed for each of the meanings given above.

(1)	*meaning of* sleeper	*parallel formations*
	person who sleeps (e.g. *heavy sleeper*)	late developer, slow reader, hard worker
	person who is asleep	boarder, fielder, speeder
	train/coach	diner, smoker
	railway tie	(= something that resembles someone asleep) reefer (a reefed sail is a rolled-up sail), trumpeter (bird species)
	delayed success	(= something which occurs after ~ing)
	piece of jewellery	(= object used while ~ing) kisser, sneaker, stroller, trotter

Note that the fact that I have no parallel for the movie or book which is a sleeper is not an argument against the point here, though it is an important point to draw attention to. The gap could, of course, simply be a failure on my part to find an appropriate word, or could arise from an incorrect gloss of what that *sleeper* implies. But if the gap is real, then we have to note that when a word is needed and there is no exact parallel to be found, the next best thing may be made to serve. In this case, *-er* serves to indicate a multitude of functions: agent in *killer*, patient in *boiler* ('boiling fowl'), instrument in *blender*, location in *diner*, point of origin in *islander*, inhabitant in *villager*, possessor in *three-decker*, and its meaning in *supper* is obscure; another function is no great extension.

All of the words in (1) have more information associated with them in our memories than can be accounted for by the linguistic form alone. This is sometimes referred to as the lack of compositionality° of morphologically complex words. A structure which is compositional can be understood on the basis of the elements which make it up and the construction in which they occur. In *The next night I took the sleeper to Paris*, *sleeper* cannot be understood solely on the basis of *sleep* and *-er* and their pattern of combination, and so is taken as non-compositional. But exemplar theory makes clear why this lack of compositionality should arise, without implying that it is a problem for the morphology.

Inflectional morphology usually is compositional, because the meanings carried by inflections are so generic, and their usage so frequent, that it is harder for them to become specialised. Nevertheless, there are occasional cases where different inflectional forms can be meaning-bearing, or at least meaning-distinguishing. For many speakers there is a distinction to be made between *indexes* for books and *indices* in mathematics or in detection: the choice of plural marker makes the form unambiguous; *brethren* is far more specific in its meaning than *brothers*, although they are both plurals of BROTHER; for some conservative speakers, *hanged* and *hung* are unambiguous, while *hang* itself is ambiguous between 'execute by hanging' and 'to attach so that the lower part is free'.

In effect, the same problem of meaning change affects monomorphemic° words in much the same way. A standard example is the word *nice*, which derives from a Latin word meaning 'ignorant' and has gone through meanings as disparate as 'silly', and 'fine (of a distinction)' before ending up as a general adjective of approval (as is mocked by Jane Austen). Although we might argue that *nice* cannot lose compositionality° because there is no construction involved, we might equally argue that *nice girl* has become non-compositional on the basis of the original meanings of *nice* and *girl*, and that *nice distinction* – to the extent that it is still used – requires the noun and the construction to create the appropriate meaning for *nice*. In this it is like *dry* used to modify *county*, *day*, *ice*, *wine* and *wit*. These changes to monomorphemic words involve changes in the way the word is perceived and categorised by speakers, and the same applies in morphologically complex words.

7.5.7 Productivity

The study of 'productivity°' deals with the extent to which morphological processes can be employed to form new words. It is clear that different affixes° or different morphological processes are productive to different degrees in different languages. Conversion° is, for example, more productive in English than might be expected on general principles – in general terms, processes which do not add form to indicate a change or addition in meaning are less favoured than ones which do (Mayerthaler 1981). In English, we have a number of negative prefixes including *a-* (in *apolitical*, *athematic*) and *un-* (in *uninhabitable*, *unlikely*). The two are not used to the same extent. There are more words with *un-* than there are with *a-*, and *un-* can often be used in places where *a-* might be expected (*atypical* and *untypical* are both found), but *a-* does not generally intrude into the domain of *un-* (so *unhappy* is found, but *ahappy* is extremely unlikely). In this particular case, the difference may be explicable by the fact that *a-* is mostly found on words derived° (directly or indirectly) from Greek, while *un-* is not so restricted. On the basis of examples like this, some authorities have suggested that productivity is limited by the constraints applied to the affix, and that the more constraints there are on a formation, the less productive it is, and vice versa.

Unfortunately, there are examples which cast doubts on this analysis. One of them is the English suffix *-ment*. Although there is some doubt as to just how productive this affix is in contemporary English (see Bauer et al. 2013), it is certainly considerably less productive now than it was in the nineteenth century. Yet it does not seem to have acquired extra constraints (unless 'don't use this!' is a constraint), and it is still very widespread in the English vocabulary – there are hundreds of nouns ending in *-ment* in any standard dictionary.

So the puzzle for a long time has been how the speaker of English knows that *-ment* is no longer productive or at least of marginal productivity, when there are so many examples of words including *-ment* in the linguistic environment. Hay (2003) made some progress with this puzzle, suggesting that to be productive an affix has to be phonologically recognisable, easily detached from its stem, and semantically transparent, but all of these things are true of *-ment* and yet it has still lost productivity. Exemplar theory may help solve this problem.

One of the things that exemplar theory demands of the human mind is that it keeps running statistics of the words it has met. Just how these statistics are kept or calculated is not something that has been explored in detail, but we can assume that the brain is in some way counting types and tokens of words and of smaller elements which are stored as types (phonemes and morphemes, but probably, as we have seen, things which are not morphemes, yet which are associated with meanings). If that is the case, then we can make a further assumption, namely that we have some kind of picture of how familiar each of the words which contains a particular affix (or other piece of form) is. One of the comments which is often made about productive morphology is that the productive affix recurs in many words which have low token counts, while non-productive morphology occurs in words with relatively high token counts (Baayen 1992). That is, given a productive affix like *-ness*, there will be some words which are very familiar (perhaps words like *frankness* and *silliness*) and a lot of words which you have not heard all that often (perhaps words like *overprotectiveness* or *globalness*). On the other hand, with an unproductive affix like the *-th* in *warmth*, every word you meet containing the affix is likely to be one you already know, and there is nothing corresponding to *overprotectiveness* and *globalness* with the *-th* suffix. As well as counts of different words (or at least some notion of frequency), the brain must store some notion of how recently words have been met. If relatively large numbers of infrequent words containing a particular affix have been recently encountered, that affix must be productive, and available for further exploitation. If the only words containing a given affix that have been met recently are familiar, there is no reason to suppose that the affix is available for further use.

7.5.8 Typology and naturalness

The school of Natural Morphology (Mayerthaler 1981) provides a series of unmarked° situations, which we expect to find in morphological system after morphological system, across languages. At the same time, it is recognised that there are language-specific markedness° conventions which may, and often do, over-rule the universal marking conventions (Wurzel 1984). So, for example, there is a universal preference for constructional iconicity°, 'more meaning requires more form', which means that affixation is preferred to conversion° or subtraction° in morphological systems. The common use of conversion in English is a language-specific exception to the general rule: it is not unexpected to find conversion, but to find it used to such a large extent is cross-linguistically odd (Manova and Dressler 2005). In a language like Tagalog, the use of infixes° is a language-specific exception to the general preference for morphological units to be continuous.

Natural Morphology is, to quite a large extent, a cognitive theory of linguistic structure. The reasons for the universally natural or unmarked situations are founded in human perception and cognition. But it has never been clear how the clash between language-specific markedness° rules and universal markedness rules is supposed to balance out in the systems of individual languages. Now, we may be able to make some suggestions.

Marked constructions can rise in any language due to random changes: the loss of final phonological segments in words, for example, can lead to the loss of suffixes (as is typically supposed to have occurred in the development of Old English into Middle English and Modern English). The subtractive° analysis of French adjectives (see Section 2.2.6) becomes possible because of the loss of final segments which used to carry the gender information in an additive way (we can still see traces of that in the spelling system of French, which is much more conservative than the phonological system). Once such unnatural effects become established in a language, they feed the system of generalisations that feed new forms. They are in the experience of speakers, while less marked options are not. Thus, until something happens to make the new system marked again, unnatural patterns can expand in individual languages.

Because there is a cognitive pressure for the natural or unmarked structure to emerge, this can happen at periods where there are no particularly strong patterns for maintaining something unnatural. The marked needs to be maintained by productive patterns, the unmarked can emerge when there are no strong constraints militating against it. New methods of word-formation in English are more likely to be additive than subtractive because, unless a subtractive pattern emerges due to phonological change, there is no pattern to support subtraction, and addition is the most widespread pattern.

Typological forces, to the extent that they exist independent of naturalness, must work in the same way: directionality of headedness (whether the head° is on the right or the left in a word) might be a typological factor in syntax or in morphology, and there is some pressure for a constant direction over certain groups of structures, and if there is no pattern of experience to force an inconsistent pattern, it can reassert itself as a grammatical feature when the social opportunity for change occurs.

Such matters may have to remain pure speculation, but they are consistent with what we observe in current systems, and consistent with the kind of approach being advocated here.

7.6 Is there anything that this kind of approach cannot explain?

I was taught linguistics as an undergraduate in the late 1960s and early 1970s, when the dominant paradigm in linguistics was transformationalism. The crucial part of that approach (or one of them) is that language is rule-governed. Given a particular set of input conditions, there is only one possible output; the same grammatical construction must always have the same form. A favourite metaphor was the algorithm: there is a path through the material which can be discovered and it leads to a unique solution.

In the approach being advocated here, it is always possible to arrive at more than one outcome. The plural of MOUSE may be *mice* or *mouses*, the negative of *typical* may be *atypical* or *untypical* or *non-typical* (perhaps even *intypical*), and we may be able to take bets on which outcome we are likely to meet, but we cannot guarantee precisely what the outcome will be on any given occasion. The image is one of seeking parallels, and a different parallel might be suggested at any moment.

Because of that, it is not clear that anything works by rule, and so there can be no certainty as to the outcome. That means we cannot write rules, in the way in which they have been written for more than half a century. Because we cannot know what the relevant parallels will be for a given speaker at a given moment, we cannot be sure about predicting outcomes, and we cannot calculate probabilities over the multiple possible parallels that are in a speaker's experience.

Although I see the benefit of this, and am convinced that it makes for a better representation of the way in which speakers operate, a representation which is more explanatory than the rules of yore, which were purely stipulative, I will admit to finding the loss of the rule something of a blow, and certainly something which requires a complete revision of the way in which I envisage the job of the linguist.

7.7 Examples

In this section, two examples of this wider notion of morphology will be discussed, San Juan Quiahije Chatino, as described by Cruz (2011), and Faroese as described by Thráinsson et al. (2004).

San Juan Quiahije Chatino (SJQ) is a Zapotecan Otomanguean language of Mexico. SJQ word stems° are largely monosyllabic, with nine contrasting vowels and twenty-one contrasting consonants. There are also fourteen contrasting tones. Tones are sometimes used grammatically, as in (2).

(2)	kwa^{MH}	's/he swept'
	kwa^{H}	'you swept'
	kwa^{HL+0}	's/he will sweep'
	kwa^{M0}	'you will sweep'

Some of the tones have very specific uses. The superhigh fall occurs only on a few expressive words, for instance. The low fall occurs only on numbers, certain potential mood verbs and adjectives. The low-super rise is found only on person-marked verbs and inalienably possessed nouns.

Examples like those in (2) can be seen as illustrating morphemes° which are realised° as tones. That is, such examples have morphemic structure, even though the morphemes are not discrete segments within the word, and are therefore potentially problematic for the classical morpheme (see Section 2.2.6). Other examples cited above are not morphemic, though. Even if the low-super rise is found only in two classes of words (and one of those is inflected), the tone does not represent a morpheme within those words. An even clearer example is that all monosyllabic loans from Spanish in SJQ contain a high tone. Not only is 'borrowed' not a morpheme, but there are many other words in SJQ which contain a high tone. Nevertheless, the high tone may be a relevant resonance° in SJQ, helping to mark a class of words. It is not clear from Cruz's description whether high tone is productive° in such words, but it is perfectly possible that it is, associated specifically with loans. Similarly, the class of number is SJQ is associated with special tone sandhi rules which do not apply to the rest of the vocabulary, but which are productive in numbers. What we see here is that tone has morphemic value in some places, but in other places it has value for the structuring of the lexicon in the speaker's mind, without that value being part of traditional morphology. The argument here is that such correlations are also important in the structure of words, even if they are not traditionally seen as morphological.

Faroese, like the closely related Icelandic, has a number of inflections which are, in the modern language, irregular and unpredictable, but which arose historically through a process of u-umlaut°, whereby a /u/ vowel in a following unstressed syllable caused a stressed vowel to become rounded. In modern Faroese, these rounded vowels have subsequently become fronted, and the /u/ which caused the change has often disappeared. Thus the plural of Faroese *barn* 'child' is *børn* 'children' (BARN originally had a *-u* suffix marking the plural), and the Faroese word for 'ark' is *ørk*. What is particularly interesting in the history of Faroese, though, is that this process has spread to created new plurals for words which never had a following /u/, but where the singular is pronounced with an /a/. In the examples in (3), the letter <æ> is pronounced [ɛa:], providing the necessary [a] sound. This innovative pattern does not apply in all dialects of Faroese.

(3)

singular	*gloss*	*plural*	*gloss*
bræv	'letter'	brøv	'letters'
knæ	'knee'	knø	'knees'
træ	'tree'	trø	'trees'

Although an [a] vowel in the singular form was originally simply a phonological item with no meaning attached, it seems that at some stage it became associated with the meaning 'singular', and motivated the umlauted plural. Here we see an example of phonological structure being perceived as meaningful (and therefore morphological in the widest sense), and being used in the production of new morphology. Standard morpheme-based morphology cannot capture such a state of affairs, but a morphology based on exemplars can.

7.8 Conclusion

Exemplar theory, based on a notion of resonances, has the possibility to provide a much more realistic view of how morphology operates in the human mind than the models which are otherwise available. If this is followed through, the domain of morphology will have to expand, because morphology then becomes the domain of generalisable structure within words rather than the analysis of those elements of words which can be said to contribute to meaning in a consistent and predictable way. Many of the theoretical problems of classical morphology then disappear, become irrelevant, or become very different in their application, and there is clearly room for more dispute as to which problems fall into which categories. Such a revisionist view of morphology will have problems associated with it, there is no doubt. However, if we want a cognitively based view of how morphology operates in the mind, this might provide us with a better option than we otherwise have available to us at the moment.

Notes and comments

There is a story that I have been told a number of times about Roman Jakobson, the Russian-born Prague School linguist who took structuralist phonology to the USA before the Second World War. In Jakobson (1941), he elaborates on the theory that children learn the phonemes° of the language they are acquiring in a largely predetermined order, with /p/ typically emerging as the first consonant and /a/ as the first vowel. Apparently, when Jakobson was giving a lecture to a lay audience on one occasion, a member of the audience commented that her child had not had /papa/ as her first word, but /kiki/. Jakobson is supposed to have replied, 'Phonetically [kiki], but phonemically /papa/.' Jakobson may have been right in insisting that contrast is independent of its phonetic realisation, but he was unhelpfully right. For the child acquiring its first language, only the phonetic categories exist, and no phonemic category can exist without a phonetic realisation. That is why phonetics and phonology are so closely linked and there can be arguments about the distinction between the two.

As a model of psychological perception and classification, exemplar theory is rather similar to prototype theory, but with the benefit, from my point of view, that it explains how prototypes can arise and that it does not require an actual psychological prototype at the centre of a cloud, merely sufficient similar exemplars to cluster. For a good introduction to exemplar theory in phonology, see Pierrehumbert (2001). Bod and Cochran (2007) define exemplar theory in the following way:

> Exemplar theory as applied to language is a theory that involves storage of linguistic experiences and that allows for production and perception as analogical generalizations over the stored memories.

This neatly captures the differences between exemplar theory (which is concrete, and generalises across memories of concrete events) and Chomskian models which are abstract and where the concrete events are (possibly inaccurate) reflections of the underlying abstract system.

Jane Austen on *nice*:

> '. . . [B]ut it is a nice book, and why should I not call it so?'
> 'Very true,' said Henry, 'and this is a very nice day; and we are taking a very nice walk; and you are two very nice young ladies. Oh! It is a very nice word, indeed! It does for everything. Originally, perhaps, it was applied only to express neatness, propriety, delicacy or refinement; people were nice in their dress, in their sentiments, or their choice. But now every commendation on every subject is comprised in that one word.' (Austen [1818] 2006: 109)

The major difficulty with the kind of approach that is advocated here is that it is probably not computable. Since resonances are personal, we cannot predict a single outcome in any case. This might have the disheartening effect that the whole theory is not falsifiable. Since the history of science post-Popper insists on falsifiability as a criterion for being scientific, this might be considered a fatal flaw. However, I don't think we have to worry too much about this. Even if we cannot predict a precise outcome for any given formation, we may be able to predict that certain outcomes are impossible, or that the range of possibilities will include a certain number of outcomes. If attested outcomes show that we are consistently wrong in such predictions, then the theory will be falsified (unless it can be shown that the route used for predictions was flawed).

Reading

For the thesis that children acquire phonology on the basis of hearing examples of speech (bottom-up processing), see Pierrehumbert (2003). There is a large literature to show that children perceive phonemic categories and do not perceive categories which are intermediate between phonemes. Pierrehumbert shows how such a result can emerge from learning from exemplars. On emergent morphology, as a theoretical position, see Archangeli and Pulleyblank (2016).

On non-morphemic resonances, see, for instance, Frost et al. (2008) who, in a summary of the literature, make the point that a word like *corner* may be analysed, counter to its morphology, as *corn* + *-er* for a few milliseconds, until a suitable interpretation is reached, at which point that analysis is dropped.

On distinguishing linguistic meaning from encyclopedic meaning and the impossibility of a distinction, see Bauer (2005). The distinction is drawn differently by different scholars, and is important within Distributed Morphology.

On compounds in general, and a more detailed discussion of some of the questions raised here, see Bauer (2017b) and references there.

Discussion questions

Some suggested answers to these questions can be found in the Answers to Discussion Questions at edinburghuniversitypress.com/rethinkingmorphology

1. Given the assumptions about the acquisition of morphology outlined above, can you explain why a native suffix like *-ful* would be unlikely to occur inside (nearer to the root than) a foreign affix like *-ation*, while the other order is possible?
2. In some varieties of English, the past tense of *swim* (and not just the past participle) is *swum*, so that we hear people say things like *I swum six lengths this morning*. In more general terms, verbs from the *swim*-class of verbs are starting to inflect like verbs of the *swing*-class. Why should this be?

3. The etymological suffix in the word *mackerel* is no longer recognised as a suffix. The same may also be true of etymological suffixes in *flicker*, *maiden* and *sparkle*. How can such a state of affairs arise?
4. Some affixes are productive, and we must assume that all of these are psychologically real. Others are not productive, but are easily analysable. For example, speakers are probably aware of the suffix *-th* in *warmth*, but may not be aware of the same suffix in *filth* and *health*. The suffix *-ment* is only marginally productive in modern English, but easily recognisable. What does this imply about the way in which morphological structure changes over time?
5. Most English transitive verbs can take the suffix *-able* to make an adjective. A number of transitive verbs in *-ate*, however, lose the *-ate* before the *-able*, so that we get *demonstrate* > *demonstrable*, *navigate* > *navigable*, though we find both *educable* and *educatable*. A full answer to what is going on here would probably take a thesis, but you should be able to speculate about what must be happening here to provide such outcomes.

Glossary

A fuller and more detailed glossary of morphology is available as Bauer (2004), which is recommended for wider explanations and definitions of morphological terms not used in this book. This glossary also includes terms from other areas of linguistics, where these might aid comprehension of the text.

ablaut	A type of apophony°, where the changes in vowel quality are not caused historically by the phonetic environment.
accusative	The case° in which the direct object of a transitive° verb typically occurs.
acronym	A word created by taking the initial letters of words in a phrase and pronouncing them as a new word: *ASCII* /ˈæski/ is an acronym derived° from the phrase *American Standard Code for Information Interchange.* Contrast with initialism°.
affix	A morph° which cannot stand alone in a sentence, but must be attached to a root° to make a word°. The major types are prefixes°, suffixes° and infixes°.
agglutination (adj: agglutinative)	A language in which each morph° typically shows a single meaning, and each meaning is typically associated with a single morph (i.e. a situation in which biuniqueness° applies) is said to show agglutination.
agreement	Matching between different words in a sentence for a particular category. There are two types of agreement: concord° and government°.
alliteration	The repetition of word-initial consonants for the sake of effect. *He has high hopes* shows alliteration of /h/.

allomorph — One of a set of morphs° which are synonymous°, phonologically similar and in complementary distribution° and thus considered to be different realisations° of the same morpheme°.

allophone — One of a set of speech sounds (or phones) which are phonetically similar, in complementary distribution° and have the same function in that they are taken to be different realisations° of the same phoneme°.

analysable — An element is analysable at a particular level to the extent that the elements available at that level are clearly distinguishable with it. The word *cats* is phonologically analysable in /k/, /æ/, /t/ and /s/, and morphologically analysable into {cat} and {s}.

animacy hierarchy — A hierarchy much used in grammatical descriptions of some languages, which treats noun phrases differently depending on the extent to which entities denoted by the noun phrase are perceived as being animate. Typically the pronoun corresponding to *I* is the most animate, humans are more animate than higher animals, higher animals more animate than insects, and all of these more animate than stones or mountains.

apophony — Alteration between vowel sounds in related words such as *foot, feet* or *long, length.* Types of apophony include ablaut° and umlaut°.

assonance — The repetition of stressed vowel sounds for effect. The expression *vim and vigour* shows assonance of /ɪ/.

backformation — The process of deleting something that is or looks like an affix° to create a new word; the new word created in this manner. *Baby-sit* is created from *baby-sitter* by backformation.

base — Anything to which an affix° is added. In *forms*, the base is *form*, the affix *-s*; in *formalise*, the base is *formal*, the affix *-ise.*

biuniqueness — A relationship between form° and meaning such that every form has a single meaning and every meaning a single form.

blend — A word created by taking the first part of one word and the second part of another, and putting them together, often with phonological overlap. *Motel* is a blend from *motor* and *hotel* with phonological overlap in the sequence /əʊt/.

booster — Anything which strengthens the force of what follows. *Very* is a booster in *very rich*. Contrast with downtoner°.

bracketing paradox — Any instance where a morphological bracketing, a syntactic bracketing or a semantic bracketing appear incompatible. In the word *ungrammaticality*, *un-* is a prefix which attaches to adjectives, and the meaning is 'the quality of not being grammatical', so on those grounds, the bracketing should be *[ungrammatical]ity*. However, the *-ity* is attached to *grammatical* because of the *-al* suffix, which leads us to expect *un[grammaticality]*. If both cannot be true at the same time, there is a paradox in the bracketing.

canonical — An approach to classification which allows individual instances to be better or less good members of the category, rather than insisting that individual items are either in the category or out of it. In English, human nouns take *who* in relative clauses and non-human ones take *which*: *The man who saw me*; *the car which crashed*. Animals are in-between. We often treat dogs as human, less often frogs. So *The frog who was sitting on the lily pad* is odd, except in a fairy-tale where animals may take on the features of humans. If 'human' is a canonical category, this is fine; if it is a category where things are either in or out, there is a problem.

case — Morphological marking on nouns, pronouns (and sometimes on adjectives and determiners) which shows the relationships between the noun phrase in which they occur and the rest of the sentence. See nominative°, accusative°, genitive°, dative°.

category, morphological — A grouping of morphological properties° on semantic grounds. The morphological category of Tense°, for example, may include past, present, future, and so on as its properties.

centre — Another name for the head°.

clipping — A word which has been phonologically shortened without changing its denotation. *Bus* originated as a clipping of *omnibus*, and *brill* is a clipping of *brilliant*.

comparative In English, the comparative is marked° with *more* (as in *more industrious*) or with the suffix *-er* (as in *bigger*).

complementary distribution Two or more items are in complementary distribution when they can never occur in the same environment (and are thus mutually exclusive), and between them they exhaust all possible environments. Items in complementary distribution are of most interest when they have the same meaning or function, and when they are somehow similar to each other. Ships and buses are in complementary distribution in that the former never travel on roads, and the latter never travel on waterways, but this only becomes relevant when they are seen as alternative manners of transporting passengers.

compositionality A construction° is compositional to the extent that its meaning can be deduced from the meanings of the elements which make it up and the meaning of the construction in which those elements occur.

compound As a first approach to the definition of a compound, we can say that it is a lexeme° whose elements are themselves lexemes, but this is not sufficient to circumscribe compounds. First, it is not necessarily clear whether *red herring* and *Oxford college* are lexemes or syntactic constructions°, second it is not clear whether *forget-me-not* counts as a piece of syntax° or a compound, and third, some scholars have more restrictive definitions of compound that, for example, include *apple cake* but exclude *apple pie* (on the grounds of stress), or include *schoolchild* but exclude *university student* (on the grounds of spelling). Most authorities agree that *blackbird* and *windmill* (for example) are compounds.

compound, tautological A compound made up of two synonyms° or a hyponym° and its superordinate°, where the meaning of one element is subsumed in the meaning of the other. *Cod fish* is a tautological compound because any cod is a fish.

concord There is concord between two (or more) elements when they must show the same value (agree°) for a particular morphological category° in the sentence.

In German, determiners and nouns must agree in gender° (amongst other things) so that we find *Das Auto* (both neuter) but *Der Wagen* (both masculine), both translatable as 'the car'.

conditioning One item conditions another if it is the determining factor in causing it to appear. Conditioning can be phonological, where some feature of the surrounding sound-system causes a particular form to appear (such the indefinite article *an* before a vowel sound, so that we have *an enemy* but *a friend*), or lexical° when a particular lexeme° causes a particular form to appear (such as the plural affix° *-en* after the lexeme OX).

conjugation class A set of verbs which share the same inflectional° paradigm°. *Swim, swam, swum* and *ring, rang, rung* in English are members of the same conjugation class, because they share the same pattern of morphological forms.

construction A unit built up of smaller units which has a function or meaning of its own. *My friends* is a construction, illustrative of a larger construction-type of noun phrase, which has functions as subject, object, and so on in a sentence.

constructional iconicity Something is iconic to the extent that its form reflects its meaning, and constructionally iconic to the extent that the amount of form in the construction reflects the amount of meaning. Constructional iconicity can be paraphrased as 'more form, more meaning'. Conversion° and subtraction° are kinds of morphology which are not constructionally iconic.

conversion Also 'zero-derivation°'. When words of different word-classes and closely related meaning share precisely the same form, we speak of conversion. *Walk* (a noun) in *I'm going for a walk*, and *walk* (a verb) in *I want to walk home* are a conversion pair in English.

dative The case° in which the person to whom something is given is typically marked.

degemination The simplification of a geminate or double consonant to a single one. Some speakers of English have a geminate in *wholly* /həʊlli/ but not in *really* /rɪəli/, where degemination has occurred.

derivation — Derivation contrasts with inflection° as one of the major branches of morphology. Derivation creates new lexemes°, while inflection creates word-forms° of lexemes. Derivational morphology is usually not fully productive°, often semantically irregular, and often changes a word from one word-class to another. The *-age* in *haulage* is a derivational affix because HAULAGE is not the same lexeme as HAUL, because *-age* is not freely added to verbs (there is no word *pullage*, for example), because *carriage* usually means a vehicle rather than an act of carrying, so the meaning is not predictable, and because *haulage* is a noun while *haul* is a verb.

derivative — A derivative is a word produced by a morphological process of derivation°.

derive — A form A derives from a form B historically if B is an older version of A in the history of the language; a form A derives from form B morphologically if B is formed by a process of derivation° from A.

diachrony (adj: diachronic) — A diachronic description of (a part of) a language describes the way in which the language changes through time. This can often be glossed as 'historical'. Contrast with synchrony°.

downtoner — A word which reduces the force of another. *Rather* in the phrase *rather unlikely* is a downtoner, because *rather unlikely* is less unlikely than *unlikely*. Contrast with booster°.

dual route — In a dual route model of producing a word, there are two ways of getting to the form: either it is looked up in memory, or it is created from basic principles.

elsewhere — The elsewhere form is the form that arises if there is no special reason to have a different one. Consider the negative prefix *in-* in English. It takes the form *im-* before a bilabial, but *in-* everywhere else (at least in the spelling). Thus *in-* is the elsewhere form.

embellishment — Embellishment is a name sometimes used for formatives° whose main function seems to be to add emotional overtones or phonological integrity rather than a particular lexical° or grammatical meaning. The *-o* on the end of *journo* (meaning 'journalist'), the *-ie* on the end of *Lizzie*, the *-ers* on the end of *preggers* (meaning 'pregnant') are examples of embellishments.

etymology — Etymology is the history of words in a given language, or the study of this. Etymologically, the word *innocent* derives from a Latin form meaning 'not harmful'. That is its historical origin, but not its current meaning. Contrast with folk etymology°.

exponence — Exponence is a term, used particularly within Word-and-Paradigm morphology, for realisation° or representation. The *-ed* on the end of English *passed* is an exponent of past tense. When several meanings are contained within a single piece of form, we speak of 'cumulative exponence'. In Latin *dominus* 'master', the *-us* is an exponent of both nominative° case° and singularity. When a meaning is realised in several different places in the word simultaneously, we speak of 'extended exponence'. In English *enlighten*, the fact that we are dealing with a verb seems to be shown simultaneously by the prefix *en-* and by the suffix *-en*.

exponent — An exponent is a form which realises° a particular morphosyntactic feature°, in a model which uses exponence°. In *discussed*, the *-ed* is the exponent of past tense. See also realisation°.

extender — A formative° which is added to a base° or to an affix,° usually for phonological reasons, to provide a longer form without extra meaning. In *Congolese*, the *-l-* is an extender.

feature — A feature is a recognisable property of some item, or the notational expression with which that property is written (usually enclosed within square brackets, [. . .]). The feature [bilabial] can be used to indicate the similarities between /p/, /b/ and /m/ in English.

feature, morphosyntactic — A recognisable and recurrent semantic property which has implications for the morphology and the syntax°. A feature such as [past tense] indicates a meaning which is marked° in the morphology, and required by the syntax, where tense must be indicated.

folk etymology — Also 'popular etymology'. A form of reanalysis where an unmotivated word is perceived as containing familiar meaningful elements. When the Spanish word *cucaracha* was borrowed into English, it had nothing within it to indicate its meaning, and it was reanalysed as having something to do with male birds, and was re-formed as *cockroach*. This contrasts with etymology°, because there is no meaning of 'male bird' in the original.

form — Any piece of orthographic or phonological material, in morphology particularly those pieces of material which have some function in the construction of words.

formative — A recurrent element in the formation of words, whether or not it fulfils the criteria for being a morph°.

free variant — Two (or more) forms which can replace each other without making any change to the unit within which they occur, and where the choice between the two is apparently random, are called free variants. The phonemes /iː/ and /e/ are free variants in the word *economic* (even though they contrast in *bit* and *bet*); *solos* and *soli* are free variants as the plural of SOLO in English.

fusion (adj: fusional) — A language in which there is cumulative and/or extended exponence° is said to show fusion.

gender — A division of nouns in some languages, based on different paradigms° being used with words which refer to beings of different sexes, but generalised to words which denote other entities. In French, when the word *livre* is masculine, it means 'book', and when it is feminine, it means 'pound (weight)'. Words of different genders frequently have different inflectional paradigms, and determiners and adjectives often also have different paradigms which have to agree° with the noun to which they belong. The term 'noun class' is often equivalent.

generality, lexical — Lexical generality is a scale of how many words a particular concept can be applied to. Plurality is more general in nouns than is sex, because there are more nouns which can be made plural than there are nouns which can reasonably be marked for sex.

genitive — A case° which typically marks possession, but which can also mark other close relationships with a noun. Both *liber puellae* 'the girl's book' and *dies irae* 'the day of anger' in Latin show a noun in the genitive case (ending in *-ae*).

government — A relationship between two items such that one determines the form of another, without itself showing a comparable marking. For example, in German the preposition *in* 'in' governs the accusative° case° when it means 'direction' and the dative° when it means 'location', so that *in die Stadt* means 'into the town' (*die Stadt* is in the accusative case) and *in der Stadt* means 'within the town' (*der Stadt* is in the dative case). In neither instance does *in* show any marking. This is one kind of agreement°.

haplology — The deletion of a sound adjacent to or close to a similar sound.

head — In syntax°, the word in a phrase which determines the kind of phrase that is involved, which can stand for the whole phrase and which denotes a superordinate° of the whole phrase; in morphology, most frequently that element in a word which determines the word-class° of the word in which it occurs.

homophony (adj: homophonous) — There is homophony when two distinct forms sound the same (have the same phonemic° make-up). *Dear* and *deer* are homophonous in English, as are the *-er* in *bigger* and the *-er* in *killer.*

hyponym — *Rose* and *tulip* are hyponyms of *flower*, *puppy* and *poodle* are hyponyms of *dog*, *bus* and *tram* are hyponyms of *vehicle.* Contrast with superordinate°.

indicative — An inflectional property° which in some languages is shown on verbs when a statement is being made.

infix — An affix° which interrupts another morph°. Khmer /sɔmnuo/ 'question' is derived° from /suo/ 'ask', and the infix, /ɔmn/, interrupts the base° /suo/.

inflection — Inflection contrasts with derivation° as one of the major branches of morphology. Inflection creates word-forms° of lexemes°, while derivation creates new lexemes. Inflectional morphology is typically fully productive°, semantically regular, and does not change the word-class° of the word to which it is added. When the inflection is determined entirely by something else in the sentence, it is called 'contextual inflection'. This is the case with instances of agreement°. When the inflection is determined primarily by the meaning, it is called 'inherent inflection'. This is usually true of tense-marking, for instance.

initialism — An abbreviation which is read as a sequence of letters: *IBM* is read as /ˈaɪ ˈbiː ˈem/ and is an initialism. Contrast with acronym°.

intransitive — A verb is intransitive when it does not have a subject complement or a direct object. In *She runs every morning*, *runs* is an intransitive verb. Contrast with transitive°.

Item and Arrangement — Also 'IA'. A view of morphology in which the morphological part of a grammar consists of a series of elements ('morphemes') and statements as to where each can occur.

Item and Process — Also 'IP'. A view of morphology in which the morphological part of the grammar consists of a series of elements ('morphemes') whose form is changed depending on where they occur.

lexeme — A word in the sense in which *is* and *are* both belong to the same word. The standard notation for lexemes is to write them in small capitals. In the case of *is* and *are*, the lexeme is BE.

lexical — To do with the lexicon° or dictionary; to do with the lexeme°.

lexicon — That part of the speaker/listener's competence in which irregularities which have to be learned are listed; this includes the fact that *cat* means 'feline quadruped', that *red herring* does not mean 'fish of a certain colour', and that *-s* can be added to nouns to make them plural. The lexicon is similar to a dictionary, though not organised in the same way.

local determinacy — Local determinacy is the principle that the phoneme° or morpheme° to which a phone or morph° belongs can be calculated by considering its neighbouring phones or morphs. This means that sometimes morphs of identical form can belong to two different morphemes, if they occur adjacent to different (sets of) morphs.

markedness	At the most fundamental level, something is marked in relation to something else if it contains an extra piece of form° (an extra morph°). Thus *inherit* is not marked for person, but *inherits* is marked for third person singular; *pretend* is not marked for tense, but *pretended* is marked. This sense of being marked is sometimes called 'markeredness', because one form has an extra marker°. Typically, languages agree in which properties are more likely to be marked in this sense, so the markedness relationships are generalisable. Because the property which carries the marker tends also to be the property which is less widely used, which is less frequent, which is learnt later by children acquiring the language, and which is most open to linguistic change, markedness has become the label to cover this wider cognitive situation. The property without the marker (the more widely distributed, more frequent, more stable property) is called the 'unmarked°' category, and is said to be more 'natural' than the property with the marker.
marker	A marker is any morphological piece of form° which represents a meaning. Usually this will be an affix° of some kind, but it can also be a change to a base°. *Prepared* and *swam* both have markers of past tense, but in *prepared* the marker is an affix, in *swam* it is the ablaut°.
minimal pair	A minimal pair is a pair of words which differ only in one place at the level at which the analysis is being carried out, and which have different meanings. Minimal pairs demonstrate the contrasting nature of the elements that differ. The words *bit* and *bet* are a minimal pair at the phonological level, and indicate that /ɪ/ and /e/ represent distinctive units and belong to different phonemes°. *Pretends* and *pretended*, which do not mean the same thing, indicate that *-s* and *-ed* contrast, represent distinctive units, and belong to different morphemes°.
monomorphemic	A monomorphemic word is a word which is made up of just one morpheme°. *Carry* and *elephant* are examples of monomorphemic words.
morph	A morph is a recurrent piece of form° associated with a fixed meaning which with other units of

	the same kind exhaustively analyses word-forms°. Various sub-types of morph are distinguished in the next entries.
morph, empty	Something which acts like a morph°, but which seems to carry no meaning.
morph, (obligatorily) bound	A morph° which can never form a word by itself, but must be attached to another morph or morphs to create a word which can stand alone.
morph, (potentially) free	A morph° which can stand on its own as an utterance.
morph, replacive	A morph which replaces another to make a difference in meaning. The difference between *foot* and *feet* could be seen as replacing *foot* with *feet* (or, possibly, as replacing <oo> with <ee>). Any analysis with a replacive morph is controversial, as it is seen as treating processes as though they were forms.
morph, unique	Something which acts like a morph°, but which is not recurrent.
morph, zero	Something which acts like a morph°, but which has no form°. Often represented by the zero-symbol, Ø.
morpheme (adj: morphemic)	A set of phonologically similar morphs° in complementary distribution° and with a common meaning; an abstract unit in which form and meaning are linked.
morphology	The study of the internal meaningful structure of words; the part of a grammar which deals with the form of words; the elements within words.
morphology, templatic	A particular view of the morphology in some languages in which a set of slots is established within the word with a set of potential fillers for each slot.
morphome	A set of forms with a predictable distribution but without a constant meaning; an abstract unit of form.
morphophonemics	Another name for morphophonology°.
morphophonology	The interface between phonology and morphology, in which the phonological form of morphological units is determined.
morphotactics	The study of the ordering of morphs° and morphemes° within the word; affix° ordering; principles or constraints affecting the way in which elements within the word are ordered.

native	(In relation to English words and morphemes.) Part of the Germanic heritage of the English language; not borrowed, especially not borrowed from French, Latin and Greek.
nominalisation	A word which is a noun derived° from a base° of some other word-class°. *Infection* is a nominalisation of the verb *infect.*
nominative	The case° which is typically used to mark the subject of a verb.
non-native	Also 'learned' or 'Latinate' (in relation to English words and morphemes). Borrowed from sources external to English, especially non-Germanic sources.
orthography (adj: orthographic)	Spelling, the system of spelling.
overt analogue criterion	A criterion for establishing morphemes° which says that that there can be no zero-morph° allomorph° of the morpheme unless there is also an allomorph which is not zero.
paradigm (adj: paradigmatic)	A set of items which can be substituted for each other at the appropriate level of analysis (e.g. in the phonological structure of the word, in the morphological structure of the word, within the sentence) and which contrast with each other at that level; an illustration of such a set of forms, intended as a pattern for learners or for classification.
phonaestheme	A sound or sequence of sounds that appears to have some, typically rather diffuse, meaning, but which does not qualify as a morph°.
phoneme	A set of speech-sound (phone) types which are phonetically similar and in complementary distribution°, whose function is to permit contrasts of meaning; an abstract unit of phonology°.
phonology	The study of the sound system of a language; the study of sound systems in general; the part of the grammar that deals with the sounds of language; the elements of the sound system and the way they are manipulated in grammar.
prefix	An affix° which occurs before the root° to which it is attached in the spoken stream of language. In *re-make*, *re-* is a prefix.
productive	A process, particularly a morphological process, is productive to the extent that it can be used in the

creation of new sequences (in morphology, of new words).

property, morphological — A value of a morphological category°: past, present and future are the properties which may represent the category Tense° in some languages.

realisation — The process or result of being made real or observable. The aspirated sound [pʰ] is the realisation of the phoneme /p/ in the English word *put*; the morph *im-* is the realisation of the morpheme {in} in *improper*. See also exponent°.

reduplication — The repetition of part or all of the form of a base° for morphological purposes.

relevance — The more a category affects the semantics of a word, the more relevant it is to that word. This has implications for morphotactics°, in that the more relevant a category is to the base°, the closer to the base it is likely to be ordered. An affix like *-dom* has a major semantic effect on its base *king*, because the meaning of *kingdom* differs considerably from the meaning of *king*. In contrast, the meaning of the *-s* in *kings* is far less relevant. Contrast with generality°.

resonance — A term devised by Hockett to denote any one of the factors which might influence the form of a word, whether in terms of formatives° or in terms of overall phonological patterning.

right-hand head rule — A proposal that the head° of a word is always the rightmost element in the word. Any such rule cannot be universal, but works well in some languages.

root — The morph° in a word which is what is left when all affixes° are removed.

scope — Consider the phrase *red panda food*. If it means 'food for a red panda', then *red* tells us only about the *panda*; to phrase this another way, *red* has scope over *panda*. If it means 'red food for pandas', then *red* tell us about the *panda food*; to phrase this another way, *red* has scope over all of *panda food*.

stem — In a British tradition, a stem is the base° to which inflectional° affixes° are added. Often 'stem' is also used for anything which has the same form as a *stem* in this first sense, independent of what type of affix is added. There is yet another use of the term when stem means any obligatorily bound° base°.

strident A strident is a sound which is produced with a hissing or hushing sound. In English, the strident phonemes are /s, z, ʃ, ʒ, ʧ, ʤ/.

structural analogy Also 'isomorphism'. To the extent that the various levels of language (phonology, morphology, syntax, semantics) are described using parallel models, parallel concepts and parallel terminology, there is a structural analogy in the descriptions of these levels. The parallels between phoneme and allophone on the one hand and morpheme and allomorph on the other indicate a structural analogy in the descriptions of these areas.

subjunctive An inflectional property, marked on verbs in some languages, which shows desire, unreality or subordination. Contrast with indicative°.

subtraction Also 'subtractive morphology'. Deleting material for morphological purposes. For example, in Murle, the word for 'rib' is *onyiit* and the word for 'ribs' is *onyii*, the word for 'warrior' is *rottin* and the word for 'warriors' is *rotti*; the plural is formed by deleting the final consonant of the singular.

suffix An affix° which follows the root° in the stream of speech. In the English word *inflectional*, both *-ion* and *-al* are suffixes.

superordinate Also 'hypernym' or 'hyperonym'. *Flower* is a superordinate of *tulip* and *rose*, *vehicle* is a superordinate of *tram* and *bus*, and *dog* is a superordinate of *puppy* and *poodle*. Contrast with hyponym°.

supine In some languages an inflectional° form which is made from a verbal base° but acts as a nominal in a sentence.

suppletion (adj: suppletive) When there are two bases in a paradigm which are not phonologically or historically related to each other, we speak of suppletion. *Go* and *went* are suppletive forms in English, as are *good* and *better*.

synchrony (adj: synchronic) A synchronic description of (a part of) a language deals with the system as it is at a single point of time. Contrast with diachrony°.

syncretism (adj: syncretic) There is a syncretism between two items if they represent distinct morphosyntactic words° but share the same form. Latin *puellae*, which can be the genitive singular of PUELLA 'girl' or the nominative plural of PUELLA, illustrates a syncretism.

synonym (adj: synonymous)
: Two items are synonymous if they share the same meaning. The English words *chiropodist* and *podiatrist* are synonyms.

syntagmatic
: Related by being adjacent in a construction°. *The* and *cat* are syntagmatically related in *I saw the cat.* Contrast with paradigmatic°.

syntax
: That part of the grammar that deals with the concatenation of words; the study of this.

tense
: Morphological marking of temporal reference (such as past or future), usually on verbs.

thematic vowel
: 'Theme' is a now rather old-fashioned term for stem°, and a thematic vowel is a vowel whose function is to create an appropriate stem form for a lexeme°.

transitive
: A verb is transitive if it has a direct object. In *He considered the point, considered* is transitive because it has a direct object *the point.* Contrast with intransitive°.

truncation
: Truncation is a form of subtraction°, the deletion of material in conjunction with the addition of an affix.

umlaut
: A type of apophony°, where the changes in vowel quality are originally conditioned by a following vowel sound. The vowel difference between *foot* and *feet* in English is an instance of umlaut.

unmarked
: Something is unmarked if it has no marker° to indicate its status. The English singular form *cat* is unmarked in relation to the plural form *cats*, where *-s* is a marker of plurality. Because unmarked forms are generally more frequent, historically more stable, and acquired earlier by children, 'unmarked' has become a label with these implications, often equivalent to 'natural' in this respect.

velar softening
: A process whereby /k/ alternates with /s/ before certain affixes. *Toxic* ends in /k/, but *toxicity* has /s/ before *-ity*, and illustrates velar softening.

voiced
: Pronounced with vibration of the vocal folds. /z/ is a voiced fricative.

voiceless
: Pronounced with no vibration of the vocal folds. /s/ is a voiceless fricative.

vowel alternation	See also 'apophony'. The use of contrasting vowels in different morphological contexts, sometimes showing a morphological contrast. The difference between *foot* and *feet* is an instance of vowel alternation, and so is the variation between /eɪ/ and /æ/ in *vain* and *vanity*.
word	As used here, 'word' is a superordinate° term for lexeme°, morphosyntactic word°, orthographic word° and word-form°. It is used when the differences between the other labels are not significant.
Word-and-Paradigm	Also 'WP'. A model of word-based morphology, in this book used as a cover-term for all such models.
word-class	Also 'part of speech'. A set of words which show comparable morphological behaviour and comparable syntactic function and distribution. Nouns, verbs and adjectives are three of the most important word-classes across languages.
word-form	A word in the sense that *is* and *are* are different words. Contrast with lexeme°.
word-formation	The creation of new lexemes° by derivation° or by compounding°. For some linguists, 'word-formation' can also be by inflection, and is then equivalent to 'morphology'.
word, grammatical	A word which has a grammatical function, such as a preposition or a modal verb. Sometimes used as a synonym for 'morphosyntactic word'°. Contrast with word, lexical°.
word, lexical	A word whose main function is to provide cognitive content, rather than to indicate grammatical function. Contrast with word, grammatical°.
word, morphosyntactic	A word defined by its place in the inflectional paradigm, as realising° the morphosyntactic properties° that are required for the syntax.
word, orthographic	A word as determined by the spelling system. If we write *rainforest*, we treat this as a single orthographic word, if we write *rain forest*, we treat it as a sequence of two orthographic words.
zero-derivation	An alternative analysis of conversion°, where one word is seen as being derived° from another by a zero-suffix, -Ø, which has no form.

References

Anderson, Stephen R. (1992), *A-morphous Morphology*, Cambridge: Cambridge University Press.

Anderson, Stephen R. (2005), 'Morphological universals and diachrony', *Yearbook of Morphology 2004*: 1–17.

Anderson, Stephen R. (2015), 'The morpheme: Its nature and use', in Matthew Baermann (ed.), *The Oxford Handbook of Inflection*, Oxford: Oxford University Press, pp. 11–33.

Anderwald, Lieselotte (2009), *The Morphology of English Dialects*, Cambridge: Cambridge University Press.

Archangeli, Diana and Douglas Pulleyblank (2016), 'Emergent morphology', in Daniel Siddiqi and Heidi Harley (eds), *Morphological Metatheory*, Amsterdam and Philadelphia: Benjamins, pp. 237–70.

Aronoff, Mark (1994), *Morphology by Itself*, Cambridge, MA: MIT Press.

Aronoff, Mark and Kirsten Fudeman (2011), *What is Morphology?*, 2nd edn, Chichester: Wiley.

Austen, Jane [1818] (2006), *Northanger Abbey*, ed. Barbara M. Benedict and Deirdre Le Faye, The Cambridge Edition of the Works of Jane Austen, Cambridge: Cambridge University Press.

Baayen, R. Harald (1992), 'Quantitative aspects of morphological productivity', *Yearbook of Morphology 1991*: 109–49.

Barnhart, Robert K., Sol Steinmetz and Clarence L. Barnhart (1990), *Third Barnhart Dictionary of New English*, [New York]: Wilson.

Bauer, Laurie (1978), 'On lexicalization', *Archivum Linguisticum*, 9: 3–14.

Bauer, Laurie (1983), *English Word-Formation*, Cambridge: Cambridge University Press.

Bauer, Laurie (1990), 'Be-heading the word', *Journal of Linguistics*, 26: 1–31.

Bauer, Laurie (1993), Review of Becker (1990), *Yearbook of Morphology 1992*: 264–8.

Bauer, Laurie (1996), 'Is morphological productivity non-linguistic?', *Acta Linguistica Hungarica*, 43: 19–31.

Bauer, Laurie (1998a), 'Is there a class of neoclassical compounds in English and is it productive?', *Linguistics*, 36: 403–22.

Bauer, Laurie (1998b), 'When is a sequence of noun + noun a compound in English?', *English Language and Linguistics*, 2: 65–86.

Bauer, Laurie (2000), 'Word', in Geert Booij, Christian Lehmann and Joachim Mugdan (eds), *Morphology: An International Handbook of Inflection and Word-Formation*, Berlin and New York: Mouton de Gruyter, pp. 147–57.

Bauer, Laurie (2001), 'Compounding', in Martin Haspelmath, Ekkehard König, Wulf Oesterreicher and Wolfgang Raible (eds), *Language Universals and Language Typology*, Berlin and New York: de Gruyter, pp. 695–707.

Bauer, Laurie (2003), *Introducing Linguistic Morphology*, 2nd edn, Edinburgh: Edinburgh University Press.

Bauer, Laurie (2004), *A Glossary of Morphology*, Edinburgh: Edinburgh University Press.

Bauer, Laurie (2005), 'The illusory distinction between lexical and encyclopedic information', in Henrik Gottlieb, Jens Erik Mogensen and Arne Zettersten (eds), *Symposium on Lexicography XI*, Tübingen: Niemeyer, pp. 111–15.

Bauer, Laurie (2012), 'Blends: Core and periphery', in Vincent Renner, François Maniez and Pierre J. L. Arnaud (eds), *Cross-Disciplinary Perspectives on Lexical Blending*, Berlin and Boston: Walter de Gruyter, pp. 11–22.

Bauer, Laurie (2013/14), 'Regularities in irregularities in English inflection', *Te Reo*, 56/57: 3–12.

Bauer, Laurie (2017a), 'Classical morphemics: Assumptions, extensions and alternatives', in Andrew Hippisley and Gregory Stump (eds), *The Cambridge Handbook of Morphology*, Cambridge: Cambridge University Press, pp. 331–55.

Bauer, Laurie (2017b), *Compounds and Compounding*, Cambridge: Cambridge University Press.

Bauer, Laurie, Rochelle Lieber and Ingo Plag (2013), *The Oxford Reference Guide to English Morphology*, Oxford: Oxford University Press.

Beard, Robert (1982), 'The plural as a lexical derivation', *Glossa*, 16: 133–48.

Becker, Thomas (1990), *Analogie und morphologische Theorie*, Munich: Fink.

Beliaeva, Natalia (2014), 'Unpacking Contemporary English Blends: Morphological Structure, Meaning, Processing', unpublished PhD thesis, Victoria University of Wellington.

Bell, Melanie (2011), 'At the boundary of morphology and syntax: Noun noun constructions in English', in Alexandra Galani, Glynn Hicks and George Tsoulos (eds), *Morphology and its Interfaces*, Amsterdam and Philadelphia: Benjamins, pp. 137–68.

Benczes, Réka (2014), 'Repetitions which are not repetitions: The non-redundant nature of tautological compounds', *English Language and Linguistics*, 18: 431–47.

Bergen, Benjamin K. (2002), 'The psychological reality of phonaesthemes', *Language*, 80: 290–311.

Bloomfield, Leonard [1933] (1935), *Language*, London: Allen & Unwin.

Bod, Rens and David Cochran (2007), 'Introduction to exemplar-based models of language acquisition and use', <https://www.researchgate.net/publication/237372296_Introduction_to_Exemplar-Based_Models_of_Language_Acquisition_and_Use> (last accessed 20 June 2018).

Booij, Geert (1996), 'Inherent versus contextual inflection and the split morphology hypothesis', *Yearbook of Morphology 1995*: 1–16.

Booij, Geert (2010), *Construction Morphology*, Oxford: Oxford University Press.

Bybee, Joan (1985), *Morphology*, Amsterdam and Philadelphia: Benjamins.

Chalmers, A. F. (1999), *What is this Thing Called Science?*, 3rd edn, Indianapolis: Hackett.

Chao Yuen-Ren [1934] (1957), 'The non-uniqueness of phonemic solutions of phonetic systems', in Martin Joos (ed.), *Readings in Linguistics I*, Chicago and London: University of Chicago Press, pp. 38–54.

Chomsky, Noam (1964), *Current Issues in Linguistic Theory*, The Hague: Mouton.

Chomsky, Noam (1970), 'Remarks on nominalization', in Roderick Jacobs and Peter Rosenbaum (eds), *Readings in English Transformational Grammar*, Waltham, MA: Ginn, pp. 184–221.

Chomsky, Noam and Morris Halle (1968), *The Sound Pattern of English*, New York: Harper and Row.

Chua Fengyi, Deborah (2016), 'Comparative Alternation in *y*-Adjectives', unpublished PhD thesis, Victoria University of Wellington.

Cruschina, Silvio, Martin Maiden and John Charles Smith (eds) (2013), *The Boundaries of Pure Morphology*, Oxford: Oxford University Press.

Cruz, Emiliana (2011), 'Phonology, Tone and the Functions of Tone in San Juan Quiahije Chatino', unpublished PhD dissertation, University of Texas, Austin, TX.

Cutler, Anne (2010), 'Abstraction-based efficiency in the lexicon', *Laboratory Phonology*, 1: 301–18.

Dirven, René (1999), 'Conversion as conceptual metonymy of event schemata', in Klaus-Uwe Panther and Günter Radden (eds), *Metonymy in Language and Thought*, Amsterdam and Philadelphia: Benjamins, pp. 275–87.

Di Sciullo, Anna-Maria and Edwin Williams (1987), *On the Definition of Word*, Cambridge, MA: MIT Press.

Dixon, Robert M. W. and Alexandra Y. Aikhenvald (2002), 'Word: A typological framework', in Robert M. W. Dixon and Alexandra Y. Aikhenvald (eds), *Word: A Cross-Linguistic Typology*, Cambridge: Cambridge University Press, pp. 1–40.

Dressler, Wolfgang U. (1985), *Morphonology: The Dynamics of Derivation*, Ann Arbor: Karoma.

Dressler, Wolfgang U., Willi Mayerthaler, Oswald Panagl and Wolfgang U. Wurzel (1987), *Leitmotifs in Natural Morphology*, Amsterdam and Philadelphia: Benjamins.

Firth, J. R. [1930] (1964), 'Speech', in *The Tongues of Men and Speech*, Oxford: Oxford University Press, pp. 139–211.

Foulkes, Paul (2010), 'Exploring social-indexical knowledge: A long past but a short history', *Laboratory Phonology*, 1: 5–39.

French, Steven (2007), *Science*, London: Continuum.

Frost, Ram, Jonathan Grainger and Manuel Carreiras (2008), 'Advances in morphological processing: An introduction', *Language and Cognitive Processes*, 23: 933–41.

Giegerich, Heinz J. (1999), *Lexical Strata in English: Morphological Causes, Phonological Effects*, Cambridge: Cambridge University Press.

Giegerich, Heinz J. (2004), 'Compound or phrase? English noun plus noun constructions and the stress criterion', *English Language and Linguistics*, 8: 1–24.

Giegerich, Heinz J. (2012), 'The morphology of *-ly* and the categorial status of "adverbs" in English', *English Language and Linguistics*, 16: 341–59.

Haspelmath, Martin (1996), 'Word-class-changing inflection and morphological theory', *Yearbook of Morphology 1995*: 43–66.

Hay, Jennifer (2003), *Causes and Consequences of Word Structure*, New York and London: Routledge.

Hockett, Charles F. [1954] (1957), 'Two models of grammatical description', in Martin Joos (ed.), *Readings in Linguistics I*, Chicago and London: University of Chicago Press, pp. 386–99.

Hockett, C[harles] F. (1987), *Refurbishing Our Foundations*, Amsterdam and Philadelphia: Benjamins.

Hornby, A. S. (2000), *Oxford Advanced Learner's Dictionary*, 6th edn, ed. Sally Wehmeier, Oxford: Oxford University Press.

Jakobson, Roman (1941), *Kindersprache, Aphasie und allgemeine Lautgesetze*, The Hague and Paris: Mouton.

Kelly, John and John Local (1989), *Doing Phonology*, Manchester and New York: Manchester University Press.

Kennedy, Benjamin H. (1962), *The Revised Latin Primer*, new edn, ed. James Mountford, Harlow: Longman.

Kibrik, Aleksandr E. (1998), 'Archi (Caucasian – Daghestanian)', in Andrew Spencer and Arnold M. Zwicky (eds), *The Handbook of Morphology*, Oxford and Malden, MA: Blackwell, pp. 455–76.

Kimball, Geoffrey D. (1991), *Koasati Grammar*, Lincoln, NE and London: University of Nebraska Press.

Kiparsky, Paul (1982), 'Lexical phonology and morphology', in The Linguistic Society of Korea (eds), *Linguistics in the Morning Calm: Selected Papers from SICOL-1981*, Seoul: Hanshin, pp. 3–91.

Klaiman, M. H. (1992), 'Inverse languages', *Lingua*, 88: 227–61.

Knowles, Elizabeth (ed.) (1997), *The Oxford Dictionary of New Words*, Oxford: Oxford University Press.

Kwon, Nahyun and Erich R. Round (2015), 'Phonaesthemes in morphological theory', *Morphology*, 25: 1–27.

Lappe, Sabine (2007), *English Prosodic Morphology*, Dordrecht: Springer.

Lieber, Rochelle (1992), *Deconstructing Morphology*, Chicago and London: Chicago University Press.

López Rúa, Paula (2002), 'On the structure of acronyms and neighbouring categories: A prototype-based account', *English Language and Linguistics*, 6: 31–60.

Lyons, John (1968), *Introduction to Theoretical Linguistics*, Cambridge: Cambridge University Press.

Maiden, Martin (2011), 'Morphophonological innovation', in Martin Maiden, J. C. Smith and Adam Ledgeway (eds), *The Cambridge History of the Romance Languages*, Cambridge: Cambridge University Press, pp. 215–67.

Maiden, Martin and Cecilia Robustelli (2000), *A Reference Grammar of Modern Italian*, London: Arnold.

Manova, Stela and Wolfgang U. Dressler (2005), 'The morphological technique of conversion in the inflecting-fusional type', in Laurie Bauer and Salvador Valera (eds), *Approaches to Conversion/Zero-Derivation*, Münster: Waxmann, pp. 67–101.

Marslen-Wilson, William (1987), 'Functional parallelism in spoken word-recognition', *Cognition*, 25: 71–102.

Marslen-Wilson, William D. and Pienie Zwitserlood (1989), 'Accessing spoken words: The importance of word onsets', *Journal of Experimental Psychology: Human Perception and Performance*, 15: 576–85.

Matthews, P[eter] H. (1972), *Inflectional Morphology: A Theoretical Study Based on Aspects of Latin Verb Conjugation*, Cambridge: Cambridge University Press.

Matthews, P[eter] H. (1974), *Morphology*, Cambridge: Cambridge University Press.

Mayerthaler, Willi (1981), *Morphologische Natürlichkeit*, Wiesbaden: Athenaion.

Mugdan, Joachim (1986), 'Was ist eigentlich ein Morphem?', *Zeitschrift für Phonetik, Sprachwissenschaft und Kommunikationsforschung*, 39: 29–43.

Nakano, Akiko (2011), 'The right-headedness of morphology and the status and development of category-determining prefixes in English', *English Language and Linguistics*, 15: 61–83.

Neef, Martin (2015), 'The status of so-called linking elements in German: Arguments in favor of a non-functional analysis', *Word Structure*, 8: 29–52.

Nida, Eugene A. (1949), *Morphology*, Ann Arbor: University of Michigan Press.

Partridge, Eric (1985), *A Dictionary of Catch Phrases*, ed. Paul Beale, London: Routledge & Kegan Paul.

Payne, John, Rodney Huddleston and Geoffrey K. Pullum (2010), 'The distribution and category status of adjectives and adverbs', *Word Structure*, 3: 31–81.

Pierrehumbert, Janet B. (2001), 'Exemplar dynamics: Word frequency, lenition and contrast', in Joan Bybee and Paul Hopper (eds), *Frequency and the Emergence of Linguistic Structure*, Amsterdam: Benjamins, pp. 137–57.

Pierrehumbert, Janet B. (2003), 'Phonetic diversity, statistical learning, and acquisition of phonology', *Language and Speech*, 46: 115–54.

Plag, Ingo (1999), *Morphological Productivity: Structural Constraints in English Derivation*, Berlin and New York: Mouton de Gruyter.

Plank, F[rans] (1994), 'Inflection and derivation', in R. E. Asher (ed.), *The Encyclopedia of Language and Linguistics*, Oxford: Pergamon, pp. 1671–8.

Press, Ian (1986), *A Grammar of Modern Breton*, Berlin: Mouton de Gruyter.

Quirk, Randolph, Sidney Greenbaum, Geoffrey Leech and Jan Svartvik (1985), *A Comprehensive Grammar of the English Language*, London and New York: Longman.

Renner, Vincent, François Maniez and Pierre J. L. Arnaud (eds) (2012), *Cross-Disciplinary Perspectives on Lexical Blending*, Berlin and Boston: Walter de Gruyter.

Rice, Keren (2000), *Morpheme Order and Semantic Scope: Word Formation in the Athapaskan Verb*, Cambridge: Cambridge University Press.

Sanders, Gerald (1988), 'Zero derivation and the overt analogue criterion', in Michael Hammon and Michael Noonan (eds), *Theoretical Morphology*, San Diego: Academic Press, pp. 155–75.

Saussure, Ferdinand de (1916), *Cours de linguistique générale*, Paris: Payot.

Schultink, Henk (1961), 'Produktiviteit als morfologisch fenomeen', *Forum der Letteren*, 2: 110–25.

Selkirk, Elizabeth O. (1982), *The Syntax of Words*, Cambridge, MA: MIT Press.

Seuss, Dr [Theodore Geisel] (1957), *The Cat in the Hat*, New York: Random House.

Štekauer, Pavol (2014), 'Derivational paradigms', in Rochelle Lieber and Pavol Štekauer (eds), *The Oxford Handbook of Derivational Morphology*, Oxford: Oxford University Press, pp. 354–69.

Stonham, John T. (1994), *Combinatorial Morphology*, Amsterdam and Philadelphia: Benjamins.

Stump, Gregory (1997), 'Template morphology and inflectional morphology', *Yearbook of Morphology 1996*: 217–41.

Thompson, Laurence C. [1965] (1987), *A Vietnamese Reference Grammar*, [Honolulu]: University of Hawaii Press.

Thornton, Anna M. (2012), 'Reduction and maintenance of overabundance. A case study on Italian verb paradigms', *Word Structure*, 5: 183–207.

Thráinsson, Höskuldur, Hjalmar P. Petersen, Jógvan í Lon Jacobsen and Zakaris Svabo Hansen (2004), *Faroese: An Overview and Reference Grammar*, Tórshavn: Føroya Fróðskaparfelag.

Toman, Jindřich (1998), 'Word syntax', in Andrew Spencer and Arnold M. Zwicky (eds), *The Handbook of Morphology*, Oxford and Malden, MA: Blackwell, pp. 306–21.

Upton, Clive, William A. Kretzschmar Jr and Rafal Konopka (2001), *Oxford Dictionary of Pronunciation for Current English*, Oxford: Oxford University Press.

Ward, Dennis (1965), *The Russian Language Today*, London: Hutchinson.

Wheeler, C. J. and D. A. Schumsky (1980), 'The morpheme boundaries of some English derivational suffixes', *Glossa*, 14: 3–34.

Wurzel, Wolfgang Ullrich (1984), *Fleksionsmorphologie und Natürlichkeit*, Berlin: Akademie.

Index